CREDIT 101

FROM **HOW TO BUILD CREDIT** AND **IMPROVE YOUR CREDIT SCORE** TO **REDUCING CREDIT CARD DEBT** AND **PREVENTING FRAUD,** YOUR **ESSENTIAL GUIDE TO USING CREDIT TO BUILD WEALTH**

CAROL POPE

Adams Media

New York Amsterdam/Antwerp London Toronto Sydney/Melbourne New Delhi

Adams Media
An Imprint of Simon & Schuster, LLC
100 Technology Center Drive
Stoughton, MA 02072

First Adams Media hardcover edition
May 2026

ADAMS MEDIA and colophon are registered trademarks of Simon & Schuster, LLC.

For information about special discounts for bulk purchases, please contact Simon & Schuster Special Sales at 1-866-506-1949 or business@simonandschuster.com.

The Simon & Schuster Speakers Bureau can bring authors to your live event. For more information or to book an event, contact the Simon & Schuster Speakers Bureau at 1-866-248-3049 or visit our website at www.simonspeakers.com.

Manufactured in the United States of America

1 2026

Library of Congress Control Number: 2025949138

ISBN 978-1-5072-2602-5
ISBN 978-1-5072-2603-2 (ebook)

CONTENTS

INTRODUCTION

If you're interested in securing a financially healthy future, having good credit is key. Your credit helps determine some of life's most important milestones, like buying a house, renting an apartment, or even getting a job. To get the money to afford these next steps, lenders need to see you're able to repay what you're borrowing. That's where credit comes in. This book helps you to understand the facets of credit and credit reports, how to raise your credit score, and more.

In *Credit 101*, you'll find simple, easy-to-understand, and up-to-date information that you can personalize to help you make the right decisions for your specific credit-related needs. Plus, you'll learn how to avoid costly pitfalls (like predatory lending), consolidate debt you may already have, and build credit when you have none. Once you understand the basics of credit, you can work on paying off debts as needed, strategize your way toward an excellent score, and learn how to keep your financial information safe. Within these pages, you'll find practical and financial advice, including:

- What your credit score is and ways to use it to accumulate wealth.
- How lenders use your score to approve or deny a loan application.
- How to read your credit report and dispute errors that are costing you.
- What loans to steer clear of.

- How to protect your identity and avoid common financial scams.
- And more!

Your credit score is sometimes influenced by things outside of your control, but the power to improve this number lies in your hands. Making changes to the way you prioritize and pay down debt, taking out the right types of loans, and slowly maintaining those upward movements puts you in charge of your credit score. Understanding how to align your life goals with your credit (and overall financial) reality is the key to long-term economic success. This book will help you navigate those complexities.

Whether you're applying for your first credit card, fixing past credit mistakes, or trying to make the most of an excellent score, this book breaks down how credit really works and offers practical information that anyone can use. No matter where you are in building, rebuilding, or taking control of your credit, this book helps to point you toward a healthy financial future. You don't need to be perfect; you just have to start. So, let's begin.

Chapter 1

The Foundations of Credit

At first glance, credit may seem complicated. However, given the right access to information and resources, you can positively impact your credit score. In this chapter, you'll start to learn the basics of credit, including what a credit score actually is, what "good credit" means, the types of debt that are out there, and how debt can be a positive (or negative) thing.

You'll also learn the first steps for succeeding in building, improving, or maintaining that score. Large purchases, after all, are a part of living; so, regardless of the types of debts you'll accrue, having good credit is not only helpful, but necessary.

WHAT IS CREDIT?

Your Financial Reputation and Ability to Borrow

In the most basic terms, credit is receiving goods or money in exchange for the promise of payment, or repayment, at a future date. Any time a consumer buys something without paying the full cost up front, they're using credit—it's a system based on trust. Some types of credit may seem obvious, like car loans, mortgages, and credit cards. But even leased furniture is considered credit, regardless of whether you plan on buying your items at the end of your contract.

Credit also refers to a consumer's ability to borrow. Whether a consumer has good credit or bad credit depends on how risky a lender deems them to be. Lenders, like banks, credit card companies, and other institutions, determine creditworthiness by reviewing factors like credit score, income, and how much debt a borrower already has. Every loan works a little differently, but generally, once a lender approves a borrower, they will give them an open line of credit (like a credit card), a lump sum of cash (like a personal loan), or funding that skips the borrower and goes directly to the entity selling the item or property (like a mortgage). Most often, borrowers must pay interest on top of their loan or line of credit, and these interest rates can be fixed or variable. Fixed rates stay the same for the life of the loan, and variable rates fluctuate with the market. Unless otherwise stated, most installment loans (like auto loans) have fixed rates. Credit cards almost always have variable rates.

HOW LENDING WORKS

When used correctly, credit can pave a path to better opportunities and greater wealth. There are a few factors to understand when using credit. In these pages, you'll learn the basics behind lending, including how interest, APR, and fees impact what you originally borrowed.

Interest versus APR

Interest is what the lender charges on top of the loan's principal amount (or the original money borrowed); it's represented by a percentage, and it's the main cost of borrowing for consumers. An annual percentage rate (APR) includes interest and fees, and it reflects the total cost of borrowing over a year's time. Lenders tend to use interest and APR interchangeably, which can be confusing because they aren't the same thing.

Simple Interest versus Compounding Interest

Almost all types of credit come with interest, but interest doesn't accrue the same way on all types of credit. Loans and cards typically have either simple interest or compounding interest. On simple interest loans, interest *only* applies to the total loan amount. Interest does not continue to build as the loan gets older. Rather, the total amount of interest due goes down as the borrower pays back their loan. So, paying a simple loan back faster will reduce the loan's overall interest.

With compounding interest, borrowers pay interest on top of interest. Credit cards are a good example of compounding interest at work. When a borrower carries a balance from billing cycle to billing cycle, they will end up paying interest on what they charged, *plus* the interest that continues to build from month to month.

Fees

Lenders also typically charge fees (additional costs), and each type of loan has its own unique fee structure. For instance, a personal loan might come with an origination fee, an auto loan could have a doc fee, and mortgage lenders usually charge closing costs. Many times, borrowers don't pay these fees out of pocket. Instead, lenders roll fees into the principal. This can help make a loan more affordable in the short term, but the more principal there is, the more interest the borrower usually pays.

A QUICK HISTORY OF CREDIT

A general understanding of how credit started and evolved will help you better grasp how credit functions today. The concept of credit and debt goes as far back as ancient Mesopotamia, around 3000 B.C. During this time, lending often revolved around food rather than physical currency. Farmers would borrow seed on credit from a palace and then pay back with their harvest (usually with interest). Mesopotamians even had a debt forgiveness system: If the farmer failed to yield a crop due to outside conditions (like poor weather), their debt was forgiven.

Credit in the modern world, however, generally started at the cash register. Until credit cards were invented, buying on credit was often as simple as starting a tab. Starting a tab was undoubtedly convenient for the borrower but risky for the shopkeeper. As borrowers started proving themselves trustworthy (or not), stores began keeping lists of customers who reliably paid their debts. Eventually, shopkeepers began selling these lists to each other, leading to an early form of data sharing. These lists led to unfair lending practices, as they didn't just include a person's borrowing history, but also based their creditworthiness on unrelated (and unethical) characteristics like their race, political affiliation, and neighborhood.

In 1841, the first U.S. credit reporting agency was created: the Mercantile Agency. However, this agency was business-to-business rather than business-to-consumer. The Mercantile Agency acted as a conduit between New York wholesalers and merchants across the country. It was incredibly risky for New York wholesalers to provide credit to a merchant 1,000 miles away. The wholesaler couldn't meet the merchant in person (an integral part of assessing creditworthiness at that time), and it had no reliable way to determine whether the merchant would be able to pay back what they owed.

The Mercantile Agency created a nationwide network of business professionals that acted as "boots on the ground" across states, investigating merchants and creating ledgers based on their findings. It would then sell these ledgers, also called reference books, to wholesalers that subscribed. Today, the Mercantile Agency still exists in an evolved form as the company Dun & Bradstreet.

America's First Credit Card

In 1949, American businessman Frank McNamara went to dinner with clients, only to realize that he'd forgotten his wallet. This gaffe inspired him to create the Diners Club card, the nation's first plastic credit card.

In the early days of credit, usury (or lending) laws were largely up to the states and/or the shopkeepers. Today, two government agencies—the Federal Trade Commission (FTC) and the Consumer Financial Protection Bureau (CFPB)—fight against unfair business practices, set national lending laws, and help define what lenders can and cannot look at when deciding a borrower's creditworthiness.

MODERN DAY CREDIT REPORTING

Nowadays, lenders rely on standardized credit reports, usually obtained through the three credit bureaus: Equifax, Experian, and TransUnion. Which report the lender uses—and how it uses that report—depends on the loan product the borrower is applying for. (These concepts are covered in the entries "The Three Credit Bureaus" and "What Is a Credit Score?") The following are the three largest credit bureaus in the United States in order of size, though there are other smaller bureaus that exist with niche specialties. It should be noted that each lender and company has the freedom to choose which credit reporting agency it uses. In some cases, it may use more than one.

- **Experian:** The largest credit bureau, known for its involvement in issuing credit cards and lending products for borrowers with good credit.
- **Equifax:** The second-largest credit bureau, known for working with utility companies, auto lenders, and specialty lending products like rent-to-own.
- **TransUnion:** The third-largest credit bureau, known primarily for its involvement with rental agencies, landlords, and lenders that specialize in working with bad-credit borrowers.

These three companies, though specializing in different things, all deal in credit. And, though the world today trades in currency rather than seeds and crops, the basic idea of credit still works the same way as it did in ancient Mesopotamia.

EXTERNAL ISSUES THAT IMPACT CREDIT AVAILABILITY

Why Qualifying for Credit Is Harder Than Ever

In the past, credit systems could be very simple. As the world got more complicated, so did lending. Today, there are no running tabs or store credit. You must submit a loan or credit card application, which is often filtered by AI or a software program rather than a human underwriter. Underwriting is the act of reviewing a loan or credit card application to determine how likely it is that the borrower will pay back their debt in full and on time.

Then, there's the broader economy to consider. When the economy is unpredictable or inflated, it's harder for lenders to assess risk. And when it's harder for lenders to assess risk, they protect against loss by raising their bar for eligibility. As you'll see in this entry, any or all of these factors can make it more difficult for borrowers to be approved for a loan.

THE ROLE OF AI AND LENDING

Many lenders today use sophisticated AI-powered underwriting programs to analyze not only credit scores but also buying behavior, income, and sometimes even alternative data like the borrower's level of education. For example, online lending platform Upstart's AI underwriting model takes more than 2,500 factors into consideration on a single loan application.

Lenders that use AI-powered underwriting say that it helps them more accurately predict if someone can truly afford a new loan or card. This can work in the borrower's favor. The more underwriting factors a lender considers means that past credit mistakes can carry less weight (since there's a larger data pool).

AI underwriting models can also make it easier for nontraditional borrowers to qualify, depending on the factors the model uses. For instance, it might be easier for a college student with no credit history to get a loan underwritten with an AI model, given that the model uses education as a scoring factor. But because the student has no credit history, qualifying will likely be harder if they apply with a bank that only uses traditional underwriting models and factors to evaluate applications.

Some argue that using AI in underwriting means less human bias, but that also means less human leniency. If the algorithm doesn't like what it sees, consider your application denied. Plus, algorithms are only as good as the data they're trained on. If an algorithm refers to data that already reflects some sort of social bias, that bias could inadvertently be applied to the loan application. Complex machine learning models operate as a sort of "black box." Because the algorithm is so intricate and uses so many data points, it's going to be hard for a human to figure out why it denied an application.

ECONOMIC UNCERTAINTY LEADS TO TIGHTER UNDERWRITING STANDARDS

When the economy is shaky or unclear, lenders protect themselves and tighten their purse strings by raising qualification requirements. They also tend to offer less-than-favorable terms to everyone except those with the best credit. It's expensive for a lender when a borrower defaults (or stops paying) on their loan or card. The lender doesn't just lose the money the borrower still owes; it also won't get the interest the borrower would have paid (and interest is the main way lenders turn a profit).

The COVID Pandemic Example

The COVID-19 pandemic is a real-world example of lenders shifting their standards during economic turmoil. Job loss was rampant due to shutdowns, and in April of 2020, the national unemployment rate was a whopping 14.7%, according to the Bureau of Labor Statistics (BLS). This led lenders to drastically pull back on credit card offers.

The Consumer Financial Protection Bureau did a study of closed (or finalized) loans and credit card applications from 2019 to 2021. In May of 2020, two months after the U.S. Centers for Disease Control and Prevention declared COVID-19 a pandemic, only about three out of ten people who applied for a credit card were approved. The month prior, that rate was close to one in two.

Taking a Risk

Why do lenders shy away from uncertainty? Because the entire lending business model is based on predicting risk. Lenders are like insurance companies in that way. A car insurance company needs to know how risky a driver is before it can determine how much to charge. It reviews factors that are largely inside a driver's control (like driving history) and ones that are more or less outside of their control (like where they live).

Instead of assessing driving risk, lenders assess financial risk. This helps them predict how likely it is that a borrower will pay back their loan. Credit score and credit history play a big role in the approval process, but so do outside factors like the economy. If the job market is weak, for example, and the borrower works in a sector prone to layoffs, the lender probably won't extend credit if it thinks the borrower will be out of a job soon. If it is willing to lend, it may charge a higher interest rate to compensate for the increased risk or to dissuade the borrower from accepting the loan.

INFLATION

Inflation is a big risk for lenders, primarily because the money they lend today could be worth less when the borrower pays it back in the future. This erosion of value has a downstream effect. As the cost of goods rises, consumer buying power goes down. This can squeeze even the most meticulously planned budgets, and people naturally prioritize essentials like groceries and utilities over credit card bills.

The Consumer Payment Hierarchy

Borrowers usually pay their mortgages first, auto loans second, and credit cards last, but this order isn't set in stone. The Federal Reserve Bank of New York found that auto loans were prioritized over mortgages during the Great Recession. Many could no longer afford their homes, so they focused on their auto debt instead.

Also, lenders aren't immune to the direct effects of inflation. When overhead costs go up, the lender's profit margin goes down. To close the gap, lenders may require higher credit scores to entice only the "safest" borrowers while simultaneously raising rates. Lenders might also pull back on how much credit they offer. A lender that typically offers loans up to $50,000 might drop its maximum amount down to $25,000. By doing so, the lender stands to lose less money if the borrower defaults.

WHAT IS GOOD CREDIT?

More Than Just a Number

Today, credit scores matter for a variety of reasons; ultimately, having a high credit score opens doors you may not have realized were shut. You need good credit to get a decent rate on a loan, rent an apartment, and pay cheaper car insurance premiums, as well as a slew of other important things for your daily life. But what's a good score, and who gets to define what's good and bad?

"GOOD" DEPENDS ON THE LENDER

Credit can be frustrating because in a lot of ways, it's subjective. According to FICO (the Fair Isaac Corporation, a data analytics company that creates credit scores), a score that falls between 670 and 739 is considered good. But a credit score is just a guideline. There is no set standard for what a lender must use as an underwriting factor—just what it can't, like your race and religion. Further, every lender "sees" your score differently. A lender that caters to good and excellent credit borrowers will view a 670 less favorably than a buy now, pay later (BNPL) app that has looser eligibility requirements.

Some lenders are more transparent about their eligibility requirements than others. Credit score requirements are often public, but lenders typically consider most of their underwriting process proprietary information. While lenders vary in transparency, their approaches to different credit profiles can be generalized by institution as follows:

- **Banks** usually require higher credit scores. Banks may be willing to work with lower credit borrowers if they have a longstanding, positive relationship with the institution and if their checking account displays responsible spending habits.
- **Credit unions** are owned by their members and are usually nonprofits. Because of this structure, they tend to have their members' best interests in mind. Credit unions don't approve every applicant, but they often carry credit products that are designed to boost or build credit.
- **Online lenders** are a mixed bag. It may be possible to get an online loan with bad or no credit, but rates can be predatory. That doesn't mean that every online lender is untrustworthy, though. Many of these lenders offer rates similar to bank loans, and some only lend to those with good (or great) credit scores.

Within each of these categories, individual institutions have their own standards for lending, and many have their own definitions of good credit.

Credit Discrimination

Lenders can't turn you down or offer you worse terms based on who you are as a person, and credit discrimination as a whole is illegal. There are a great number of laws in place to disallow unfair lending practices; some of which are:

- **The Equal Credit Opportunity Act (ECOA)** prohibits lenders from using your race, color, religion, national origin, sex, marital status, age, or public assistance use as underwriting factors.
- **The Fair Housing Act** offers similar protections, but for housing, homeowner's insurance, and banking. For example, this act

means that landlords can't refuse to rent to you because of your race or other similar factors.

- **The Fair Credit Reporting Act (FCRA)** protects your information and gives you the power to dispute information on your credit report. The FCRA also ensures that you're informed when a credit card company, loan company, employer, or insurance company takes an adverse action based on your credit report (such as offering an increased car insurance premium based on the information found on a soft credit hit).

Knowing what resources there are to protect you will help immensely when applying for credit and paying back your debt.

"GOOD" DEPENDS ON THE TYPE OF LOAN

What a lender considers "good" credit usually depends on the specifics of the loan, including how much the borrower is requesting and why, the loan's term, and whether collateral or a down payment is involved. For example, a mortgage is harder to qualify for than an auto loan. Mortgages usually last for fifteen to thirty years and involve hundreds of thousands of dollars or more. In contrast, car loans cap out at seventy-two or ninety-six months (six to eight years). The longer a loan is open, the more chance the borrower has to fall behind on payments. And the larger the loan, the more the lender stands to lose if that should happen.

Collateral is also something to consider. Collateral is valuable property that the lender can repossess if the borrower stops paying. This helps the lender hedge its bets and lower its risk. On a mortgage, the home being financed serves as collateral. For auto loans, it's the car. Loans with collateral can be easier to qualify for than credit cards. If a borrower stops paying on most types of credit cards, the lender has nothing it can repossess to recoup some of its loss. And for loans that require a down payment, a larger contribution might compel a lender to accept a lower score. More money down means a smaller loan, and a smaller loan is less risky for the lender. The borrower has skin in the game and may be more likely to pay on time to avoid losing their down payment through repossession.

Even how a borrower plans on using a loan can make or break an application. If a borrower's score is on the low end of good, a lender may be more apt to approve a personal loan for debt consolidation than it would be for a vacation. When someone begins debt consolidation (the act of taking out one loan to pay off several other debts), it shows that they're serious about taking control of their finances. On the other hand, a person who is more financially stable may be more likely to save up for a vacation rather than take on debt to fund it.

"GOOD" DEPENDS ON YOUR OVERALL FINANCIAL HEALTH

Your credit score is just a small snapshot of your financial health. Lenders also look at factors that aren't directly related to your score, such as your debt-to-income ratio (DTI). DTI is not technically part of your credit score, but lenders can calculate it by looking at your credit report. DTI measures how much debt you have compared to how much you make before taxes. Many lenders consider a DTI ratio at or above 36% as a red flag. To them, it means you may already have more debt than you can handle.

Calculate Your DTI

To calculate your DTI, add up your monthly debt payments and divide them by your pretax monthly income. Here, debt means credit card payments, mortgage or rent payments, personal loan payments, and other debt tied to a credit product. Don't include living expenses like groceries, utilities, and entertainment.

How long the borrower has been with their current employer is also important. Lenders look for stability. If a borrower job hops every couple of years, the lender might view them as less reliable. Depending on the type of loan, the lender might also ask for a running bank statement (detailed transaction history) and a list of assets to make sure the borrower has a steady source of income and a nest egg in case of unexpected job loss.

TYPES OF DEBT

Know Your Loan Before Signing the Dotted Line

When someone has debt, that simply means that they owe something (like cash, goods, or services) to another party. However, not all debt is the same, and each type is linked to a different financial product. Remember: The debt that you take on impacts your credit, as do the payments you make toward that debt. Knowing the differences between types of debt and how you accrue them is key to understanding how credit really works; you'll learn about all of this in detail in this entry.

SECURED DEBT VERSUS UNSECURED DEBT

The first types of debt we'll review are secured and unsecured debt. These types of debt are classified based on their use of collateral, and both have pros and cons based on the factors described here.

Secured Debt

Secured debt is backed by collateral, which makes it easier to qualify for, as mentioned in the previous entry. To back something with collateral, the lender puts a lien on the collateral. A lien is a legal claim that gives the lender the right to repossess or seize the collateral, although the borrower is still the owner of the property. For example, if a borrower falls too far behind on their car payments, their finance company (or lienholder) can repossess (or take back) the car. Mortgage companies, on the other hand, won't "take back" the home if the homeowner stops making payments, as the mortgage company never had possession of the home to begin with (it just provided the financing the homebuyer needed to complete the purchase). Instead, the mortgage company will foreclose (or sell) the property to another buyer to make back its losses.

Most of the time, the collateral is directly tied to the loan, like in the car and mortgage lender examples. But on some loans, the collateral has nothing to do with the reason for the loan. Pawnshops, for example, frequently accept jewelry, electronics, musical instruments, or anything else of value. Other than auto loans and pawnshop loans, some other popular forms of secured debt include mortgages, home equity loans, and home equity lines of credit (HELOCs).

Unsecured Debt

Unsecured debt is not tied to collateral. Instead of repossession, the lender will "charge off" the debt if the borrower defaults. This means the lender will stop attempting to get the borrower to pay. Instead, the lender will write it off as a business loss. Then, the lender may sell the debt to a debt collection agency, usually for pennies on the dollar. Depending on how much is owed, the lender could also take the borrower to court to get permission to garnish the borrower's wages. Credit cards, medical bills, student loans, most personal loans, and personal lines of credit (PLOCs) are unsecured.

Balancing Risk with Reward

Secured loans are lower risk for lenders, so they come with lower rates. Conversely, unsecured loans tend to have higher rates but are lower risk for the borrower. The lender can't repossess collateral to recoup losses if the borrower falls behind.

REVOLVING DEBT VERSUS INSTALLMENT DEBT

In addition to being secured or unsecured, debt can also be revolving or part of an installment, which defines how funds are borrowed and repaid. These two types of debt are used for very different purposes, each having their benefits for the types they're used in.

Revolving Debt

Credit cards, HELOCs, and PLOCs are forms of revolving debt. Also called open-ended credit, revolving debt gives borrowers continued access to money, and paying back what is owed frees up more credit that can be used again up to a certain limit. As long as the borrower is within their credit limit, they can generally borrow as often as they'd like. The borrower's monthly payments will go up and down based on how much they charged during their billing cycle and their interest rate at the time.

Often, interest compounds on revolving debt. This means that interest continues to grow on what is owed, and that interest gets added to the loan's principal or the card's balance. Once this interest is added to the principal or balance, it also accrues interest. In other words, borrowers pay interest on their interest with compounding debt. Interest rates are usually variable. Variable interest rates are tied to market conditions, but, contrary to popular belief, they aren't directly dictated by the Federal Reserve, either. Instead, they're usually connected to *The Wall Street Journal* prime rate. This is the average rate that most lenders are currently giving to their most creditworthy borrowers. While the Federal Reserve rate can indirectly impact the prime rate, its primary purpose is to set the price that banks charge each other for loans—not dictate the pricing the banks and lenders charge consumers. For consumers, the main takeaway here is that monthly payments fluctuate on variable interest debt, based on the current interest rate that the lender is charging at any given time.

Installment Debt

Installment debt is also called closed-ended credit. Mortgages, home equity loans, auto loans, and personal loans are types of installment debt. Installment debt provides funds as a lump sum. Sometimes, the funds will go directly to the borrower, as is the case with a personal loan. Other times, the funds skip the borrower and go to a person or entity selling property, like with a mortgage. After the loan is finalized, the borrower will repay in equal monthly payments over a certain period of time (called a loan term).

Installment debt usually has fixed interest rates; the interest rate at the start of the loan will remain the same until the end of the loan. Interest *usually* doesn't compound on installment debt. Instead, the lender calculates how much interest the borrower will pay based on how much is left on the loan. If the borrower pays off their loan faster than their loan term allows, they will pay less total interest.

The Long and Short of Loan Terms

Loan terms are usually expressed in months or years. The longer a loan term is, the more time you have to spread your balance across. This leads to a lower monthly payment. However, the longer it takes you to pay back your debt, the more overall interest you'll pay.

GOOD DEBT AND BAD DEBT

Not All Debt Is Created Equal

There's a common myth that one should avoid borrowing money at all costs. After all, borrowing isn't free, and having an excess of debt can stop you from reaching other financial goals. Yes, taking on debt is serious business. But with proper planning, borrowing for the right reasons can be a strategic way to build wealth and credit. Understanding different types of debt can help you choose the product that best suits your needs or whether you should take on debt at all. It can also help you avoid expensive loans or cards that could lead you to fall behind on payments, damaging your credit score and your ability to borrow down the line.

GOOD DEBT AS AN INVESTMENT IN YOUR FUTURE

Good debt helps a borrower increase their net worth. To figure out whether debt is good or bad, you must weigh the cost of borrowing against the potential for future earnings. In general, loans or credit that help boost your education level, living situation, or business opportunities, or that increase the value of a tangible item, can be good debt. Consider the following examples.

Student Loans

A student loan can be a form of good debt: Go to college, get a degree, and make more money. But there are some factors to consider before automatically labeling a student loan as good debt. One is the earning potential of the field of study the student is interested in. It may not be wise to go into debt to get a degree in a sector that doesn't show much growth or earning potential. Also, tuition costs are something to think about. Unless the student is planning on entering a highly competitive or specialized field, getting a smaller student loan and going to community college for the first two years can be a huge money saver. And the more money the student saves, the larger return they'll get on their investment.

Importantly, though, a student loan (specifically, a federal student loan) can quickly turn from good debt to bad if the borrower doesn't understand how interest accumulates on what they borrowed. Federal student loans use simple daily interest. That means that the principal earns interest every day. If it's a subsidized loan, then interest does not accrue while the student is in school. On unsubsidized loans, it does. Either way, when it's time for the student to start repayment, the interest is capitalized, or added to the loan's principal. Then, this larger amount accrues interest as the student repays their loan, likely over many years or decades.

Mortgages

A mortgage can be another type of good debt, but it depends on the housing market, the neighborhood, the condition of the home, and whether the borrower is overstretching their budget. Under the right circumstances and with proper upkeep, the property could rise in value. This increase could outweigh the interest the borrower paid on the mortgage if they decide to sell.

Business Loans

Taking out a loan to start a business can have a huge payoff, but opening a business is a serious commitment, and a serious risk. Unless the borrower went to business school or has another form of experience, it's a good idea for them to meet with a consultant to see how viable the business could be. A business plan is a must, as is targeting the right type of loan. Government-backed Small Business Administration (SBA) loans typically have the friendliest rates and terms, but the process can be arduous and lengthy.

Home Renovation Loans

According to the *Journal of Light Construction*, simply replacing a garage door has a 268% return on investment, on average. If the borrower qualifies for a reasonable APR, borrowing for home renovations could pay off big, assuming the borrower sells their house down the line.

BAD DEBT IS UNNECESSARY OR EXPENSIVE

If good debt increases a borrower's net worth and credit score, then bad debt does the opposite. Rather than coming out ahead, the borrower ends up spending more on interest than the purchase was worth. Bad debt comes in a few forms, including:

Unnecessary Debt

Taking on debt for nonessentials can be a quick way for a borrower to end up in the red, and for no good reason. Still, it's important to note that something doesn't always need to have tangible value for it to be essential. You don't *have* to throw a traditional wedding to get married. But if the memories and celebration are worth it to the borrower, a wedding loan could be good debt as long as the borrower is at peace with the interest they'll pay.

Expensive, Short-Term Debt

Most lending laws (or usury laws) are handled at the state level, and there is no one federal law that strictly defines predatory lending. Even so, financial experts generally agree that rates above 36% are predatory. The same goes for loans that have short, weeks-long repayment terms. It can be hard, if not impossible, to keep up with loan payments when there's one due every week or two.

Special Rules for Military Members

The Military Lending Act (MLA) prohibits lenders from certain predatory practices, including charging APRs above 36% on some types of loans. The Department of Defense conducted a study and found that high-interest payday loans have a negative impact on military readiness.

Expensive debt is usually a byproduct of an emergency, poor credit, or impulsive spending. An emergency fund and solid budget are essential to avoid excessively high rates. If a borrower has less-than-perfect credit, it would make sense for them to improve their credit before borrowing, assuming they have the luxury of time.

Debt for a Depreciating Asset

Using a loan or card to buy an item that will go down in value can lead to bad debt. For example, using a loan to buy a brand-new car is often considered unwise. Kelley Blue Book states that new cars usually decrease in value by about 20% in the first year of ownership.

This is not to say that buying a brand-new car will always lead to bad debt. If the buyer qualifies for a 0% APR deal or pays their loan off quickly (effectively reducing the amount of interest they'll pay), the peace of mind that comes with a brand-new car could be worth it. Still, buying a certified pre-owned vehicle might be a better deal. The car has already depreciated some, so the asking price will be lower. And although certified pre-owned cars might not have that new car smell, they do typically have warranties similar to those of a new car.

Cars aren't the only assets that depreciate. A home can be a depreciating asset if it's located in an undesirable area or if the homeowner doesn't keep up with repairs. Cell phones and electronics also almost always depreciate in value over time. Anything you buy could be a depreciating asset, making it important to research before financing or taking on debt.

Chapter 2

Credit Reports and Credit Scores

It can be easier to understand the link between credit bureaus, credit reports, and credit scores by thinking about them in terms of school. First, there's the credit bureau. In this analogy, a credit bureau is like a school's record or registrar's office. It collects your grades (credit history) from your lenders and organizes this information into a transcript (credit report). Then, credit scoring companies, like FICO (Fair Isaac Corporation) and VantageScore, synthesize the data on your credit report to create your credit score (or your grade point average).

Understanding how your credit score is generated will help you identify what changes (if any) you need to make to level up your credit profile and, in turn, your borrowing power. It's also essential that you know how to read your credit reports. Credit reporting errors are common, and you can't flag something as an error if you aren't sure what should show on your report in the first place. Throughout this chapter, you will learn the various elements of what goes into the reports and scores, as well as the three major credit bureaus that issue the reports.

THE THREE CREDIT BUREAUS

Credit Report Creators

Credit reports are created by credit bureaus, also known as credit reporting agencies (CRAs). CRAs don't take payments, lend money, or process (approve/deny) applications. Instead, these for-profit companies take consumer data that they receive from lenders and use it to create credit reports. Understanding what a credit bureau is and what it does can help you identify errors faster. These are the entities that you will contact if you need to dispute information on your credit report.

THE BIG THREE: EQUIFAX, EXPERIAN, AND TRANSUNION

Borrowers have credit reports from several different reporting agencies, but the three largest CRAs in the United States are Equifax, Experian, and TransUnion. Why are there multiple bureaus? Although these three competing companies collect similar data, each organizes the data in a different way. Lenders choose which bureau(s) to send data to, when that data gets sent, and which scoring model (FICO or VantageScore) it will use to calculate a credit score from a borrower's credit report. Some lenders use two or even all three of the bureaus to calculate scores.

Equifax

Although lenders, creditors, and companies have total control over which credit bureau they ask to pull data from, Equifax is often used by utility companies to determine whether they will require a new customer to put down a deposit to start services. Equifax also partnered with FICO to create the Beacon score, an older scoring model that is now mostly known simply as a FICO Score. In general, auto lenders also tend to favor Equifax.

Initially called the Retail Credit Company, Equifax was formed in 1899 by two Tennessee grocers. These grocers kept track of customers who bought goods on credit, and they soon realized that the data they were compiling was more valuable than the groceries they sold.

Today, Equifax is not only one of the big three credit bureaus, but it is also the first credit bureau to use an explainable neural network (AI plus advanced machine learning) to help make underwriting decisions. That means it was the first to be able to explain the why behind its AI-based credit decisions, which is important from a legal standpoint—the Equal Credit Opportunity Act requires credit bureaus to explain why they made an adverse underwriting decision.

Experian

Experian is a popular bureau for credit card issuers and is the largest credit reporting bureau, while Equifax is the second largest. American Express, Chase, Capital One, Citi, Discover, and Wells Fargo all use Experian primarily (or in conjunction with the other bureaus) when a consumer applies for a credit card. But credit card issuers aren't the only entities that use Experian. As the largest bureau, Experian is used widely across the field of lending.

Experian is the product of a few UK and American companies evolving and eventually merging. In the beginning, some tailors in London started trading customer information and debt records in 1803. This led to the 1826 formation of the Society of Guardians for the Protection of Tradesmen against Swindlers, Sharpers and Other Fraudulent Persons, later called the Manchester Guardian Society. In 1900, home mail-order company Universal Stores was formed, later becoming Great Universal Stores Limited (GUS). The Manchester Guardian Society was later absorbed into GUS. This eventually became Experian UK.

Meanwhile in America, a man named Jim Chilton started the Merchants Credit Association in 1897. This eventually became the start of Experian's American operations. Decades later, automotive and aerospace company TRW Inc. acquired the Merchants Credit Association, and in 1968, TRW acquired a company called Credit Data Corporation. This helped TRW to become one of the biggest data collection and credit reporting companies in the country. In fact, credit reports were commonly referred to as TRW reports. Finally, in 1996, GUS bought TRW's credit reporting division, and from this merger, Experian U.S. was born.

TransUnion

TransUnion may be the smallest of the largest credit bureaus, but it still collects data on over one billion global consumers. Rental agencies and landlords frequently turn to TransUnion when deciding whether to work with a prospective tenant. Also, most consumer-facing free credit scores (like those from Credit Karma) are derived from TransUnion reports.

TransUnion got its start in 1968 as the parent company for a railyard leasing business called the Union Tank Car Company.

Quickly, TransUnion began to collect credit information, and in 1969, it expanded its data-collection operations by acquiring the Credit Bureau of Cook County. At the time, the Credit Bureau of Cook County held credit information for 3.6 million Americans. TransUnion also pioneered the automated tape-to-disk transfer, which moved consumer data from magnetic tape to magnetic disk. This allowed for quicker, easier access to files and, ultimately, faster credit reviews. By 1988, TransUnion was a nationwide CRA, and it became a publicly traded company on the New York Stock Exchange in 2015.

CRA-Related Protections Granted by the FCRA

The Fair Credit Reporting Act states that any entity that takes an adverse action against you during a credit application must tell you why, and which CRA the information came from. You also have the right to dispute incorrect information the CRA has listed on your credit report.

ALTERNATIVE CREDIT BUREAUS

Equifax, Experian, and TransUnion aren't the only credit bureaus, but they are the most widely used. There are dozens of CRAs, each specializing in certain data and credit products. Two of the more common ones are Innovis and Clarity Services.

Innovis

Innovis is considered the fourth major CRA, although it's used far less than Equifax, Experian, and TransUnion. Innovis specializes in identity verification and fraud detection. Lenders typically use it as a prescreening tool at the start of a credit application.

Clarity Services

Clarity Services is a product of Experian, and it's geared toward borrowers with bad or no credit. Payments that typically don't "count" for the big three do for Clarity Services, including payday loans, car title loans, and rent-to-own services like Rent-A-Center. When a lender offers a credit product with no credit check, that usually means that it uses Clarity Services rather than one of the big three CRAs to determine a borrower's creditworthiness.

HOW TO READ A CREDIT REPORT

What Do Your Reports Say about You?

From opened and closed cards to on-time and late payments, a credit report gives a detailed account of your borrowing history. Knowing how to decipher your credit report will help you spot and dispute credit reporting errors, a skill that can potentially boost your credit score. This entry walks through the many different contents of a report, providing context for each.

CONTENTS OF A CREDIT REPORT

Your credit report is a living document that changes with your borrowing behavior, but it doesn't update in real time. Every lender decides when it will report your payment history to the credit bureaus, but most do so every thirty to forty-five days. Also, not all lenders report to all three bureaus. Some might not report at all. Generally, though, established borrowers have a separate credit report for each of the big three bureaus. Credit reports don't look the same across bureaus, even for the same borrower; bureaus can use different terminology to describe the same thing, and each could contain slightly different information. But generally, a credit report includes the following information.

Personally Identifiable Information (PII)

PII includes your name, aliases, current and former addresses, date of birth, Social Security number, employment information, and phone number. PII does not impact your credit score. Lenders use it to make sure you are who you say you are and that the information that you're providing on your application is true

Public Records

Prior to 2017 and 2018, the public records section of a credit report provided details about certain legal actions taken by or against the borrower. It was where lenders could see whether a borrower had filed for bankruptcy, whether the government had put a lien on a borrower's property due to back taxes, or if the borrower had been sued in civil court. But today, almost the only thing a lender will see are past bankruptcies.

In 2015, thirty-one state attorney generals investigated the accuracy of credit reporting, and based on their findings, the three credit bureaus agreed to a settlement referred to as the National Consumer Assistance Plan (NCAP). The NCAP standardized how credit reports display PII, what information is required before a civil judgement or tax lien can be shown on a report, and how often public records must be updated on a credit report. As a result, almost all civil judgements were removed from credit reports in 2017. In 2018, Equifax, Experian, and TransUnion agreed to remove all tax liens.

NCAP's Impact on Credit Scores

According to the Consumer Financial Protection Bureau, the NCAP had little direct impact on credit scores. Before the NCAP, 6% of consumers had a tax lien or civil judgement on their credit report. After most of these were removed, only about 4% of affected consumers had their credit score jump enough to qualify for a better credit tier.

Adverse Accounts

Late, missed, and charged-off payments are found under the adverse accounts section of a credit report. A charge-off is a debt that is so beyond its due date that the lender has sold it to a debt collection agency. These actions are typically listed for seven years, but CRAs do keep older debts on record and may release the information if you apply for more than $150,000 in credit or life insurance above $150,000 in coverage, or if you apply for a job that pays more than $75,000 a year.

Satisfactory Accounts

Accounts are considered satisfactory when they're current and when the borrower has made all of their payments as agreed. This section of a credit report also lists what types of accounts a borrower has (revolving credit like credit cards or installment debt like an auto loan, for instance), the date the account was opened, whether there is another borrower on the account, and repayment terms. Positive closed accounts typically remain on your report for ten years.

Credit Inquiries

FICO and VantageScore use the credit inquiries portion of a credit report to calculate your new credit and recent credit score factors. New credit (used by FICO) and recent credit (used by VantageScore) measure how many recent credit lines you have opened and how many credit accounts you've applied for within the last two years. Hard and soft inquiries are also listed here, although hard inquiries are the only ones that impact credit scores. This book covers hard and soft inquiries in more depth later on in this chapter under the "Hard and Soft Credit Inquiries" entry.

OTHER REPORTS THAT INFLUENCE YOUR FINANCIAL OPPORTUNITIES

As discussed, each of the major credit bureaus has its own credit report. These are the only credit reports that influence your FICO and VantageScores, but other specialized reports exist. Although these specialized reports don't influence your credit score, they can impact other major financial milestones, like opening a bank account or getting lower insurance rates. This is by no means an exhaustive list, but some specialized reports include:

- **ChexSystems** and **Early Warning Services (EWS)** track overdrafts, bounced checks, bank fraud, and account activity.
- **Cotality**, **SafeRent Solutions**, and **TransUnion SmartMove** are credit reporting agencies that landlords use to screen tenants.
- **National Consumer Telecom & Utilities Exchange (NCTUE)** is a database that utility, cell phone, and internet companies use to keep track of customer account activities.
- **Comprehensive Loss Underwriting Exchange (CLUE)** and **motor vehicle reports (MVRs)** keep track of drivers' claim, accident, and driving histories.

Regardless of the credit report, each has its uses and are important in influencing parts of your future (financial and otherwise).

WHAT IS A CREDIT SCORE?

The End Result of Your Credit Report

Credit scores are one of the main ways that a lender determines risk. The more creditworthy the borrower, the higher their score. There are two main types of credit scores, FICO and VantageScore. Under the FICO Score and VantageScore umbrellas, you'll find industry-specific scores that apply only to certain credit products, like the FICO Auto Score. And as credit evolves, FICO and Vantage-Score continue to release updated credit scoring models, which lenders can choose to implement (or not) at their leisure.

FICO SCORES

To standardize lending and level the playing field for borrowers, analytics company Fair Isaac Corporation invented the FICO Score in 1989. Before FICO Scores, lenders often used arbitrary and inconsistent factors to determine a borrower's creditworthiness. Not only was this unfair, but it also made it hard for a borrower to understand whether they had a shot at the loan or card they wanted before actually applying. FICO Scores are determined by an algorithm, and this algorithm predicts how likely it is that a borrower will default within two years of the loan or card's inception. A default happens when a borrower misses payments for ninety days or longer.

Credit Scores Around the Globe

Many other countries also have their own versions of credit scores, including Australia, Canada, Germany, Japan, and Spain—and there is no exchange rate. Borrowers who move internationally usually must start over and build credit in their new home country.

FICO TODAY

Today, FICO Scores are the most commonly used credit scores across lenders, and more than forty countries have adopted the model. There are dozens of distinct FICO Scores, each used for different types of credit products; an auto loan lender will look at your FICO Auto Score, while a credit card company will use your FICO Bankcard Score. FICO also releases new scoring models as credit products evolve, such as its FICO Score 10 BNPL model, the first credit scoring system to include buy now, pay later payments when calculating a score.

FICO Score Credit Tiers

General FICO Scores range between 300 and 850, and industry-specific scores range from 250 to 900. Each range is assigned a credit tier (or band), which is a general classification of how risky a borrower is. According to the most recent data, the average FICO Score in the United States is 715.

FICO SCORE CREDIT TIERS		
CREDIT SCORE RANGE	**CREDIT TIER**	**WHAT IT MEANS**
Less than 580	Poor or bad	You probably won't qualify for most loans and cards.
580 to 669	Fair	You might qualify for some loans and cards, but not at the best terms.
670 to 739	Good	You probably have access to mainstream lending products with competitive rates.
740 to 799	Very good	You should qualify for low rates on most credit products.
800 to 850	Excellent	You'll probably qualify for the best rates depending on other factors (like income).

VANTAGESCORES

Created in 2006 by Equifax, Experian, and TransUnion (the three credit bureaus), VantageScore is a newer credit scoring model, at least compared to FICO. If you've ever checked your credit score for free, you likely have experience with VantageScore—most free credit check services pull it rather than FICO. The goal of VantageScore is to help a more diverse population access credit. VantageScore claims that it can generate a credit score for 94% of adults, which is thirty-three million more than the classic FICO Score.

The newest VantageScore 4.0 model is generally more lenient and considers more data points than the classic FICO Score, such as rent and utility payments. Borrowers can also generate a VantageScore in as little as one month, but a classic FICO Score requires at least six months' worth of history on at least one account. Further, VantageScore 4.0 does not hold paid collections against borrowers. The same is true for a few newer FICO models, like FICO 9, FICO 10, and FICO 10T. But credit card issuers, car loan lenders, and personal loan lenders more commonly use FICO 8. With FICO 8, a paid collection account can impact a FICO Score for up to seven years.

VantageScore Credit Tiers

Some older VantageScore models run from 501 to 990, but in the spirit of simplification, VantageScore updated its credit ranges to match FICO's in its most recent models. Ranges run from 300 to 850, but credit tiers are a little less granular, since VantageScore has four tiers compared to FICO's five. Still, each means about the same thing. The average VantageScore in the United States is currently 702, the equivalent of a good FICO Score.

VANTAGESCORE 3.0 CREDIT TIERS		
CREDIT SCORE RANGE	**CREDIT TIER**	**WHAT IT MEANS**
300 to 600	Subprime	You may only qualify for predatory lending products.
601 to 660	Near prime	You could qualify for a loan or card, but rates will be high.
661 to 780	Prime	You should qualify for most loans and cards at competitive rates.
781 to 850	Superprime	You'll likely qualify for the best rates and terms.

You might not know what scoring model the lender or credit card company uses when you apply, although most use FICO. Many lenders consider what model they use and their minimum credit score requirements as proprietary information. For that reason, it's essential that you know how both FICO and VantageScore work.

HOW CREDIT SCORES ARE CALCULATED

Know the Why Behind the Numbers

Checking your credit is a great habit, but knowing what goes into your score will help you take it to the next level. Understanding how your score is calculated will help you figure out what areas of your credit profile you should put the most focus on. Taking uneducated guesses about improving or maintaining your credit score can lead to slow results. Slow results can be demoralizing, frustrating, and may prevent you from reaching your potential. FICO Scores and VantageScores are calculated in similar ways, but each has a few distinct differences detailed in this entry.

FACTORS THAT DETERMINE A FICO SCORE

There are five factors that determine a FICO Score, each with different weights. The higher the factor's weight, the greater the impact it has on your score.

Payment History

Payment history makes up 35% of your FICO Score, making it the single most important factor for FICO. Payment history is just what it sounds like: It measures whether you make your debt payments on time. If you've ever been late, it tracks how late you were.

It also considers past bankruptcies, how many times you've paid late, and how long it's been since you've made a late payment.

Amounts Owed

Amounts owed makes up 30% of your FICO Score. While it's not quite as impactful as payment history, it's close. Accounts owed tracks your credit utilization ratio. This is how much revolving credit you're using compared to how much you have available. For closed-end (installment) credit, it considers how much you still owe compared to how much you've paid off.

Length of Credit History

Length of credit history makes up 15% of your FICO Score. This factor looks at the age of your oldest account, the age of your newest account, and the average age of all your accounts combined. It also examines how long certain accounts have been open. A mortgage with twenty years of on-time payments will have a more significant impact than a twenty-five-year-old store card that is rarely used.

Credit Mix

Credit mix makes up 10% of your FICO Score. Credit mix measures the diversity of the credit accounts you have. A borrower successfully managing an auto loan, a mortgage, and a credit card will have a higher credit mix score than someone who only has a credit card.

It's In the Mix

It's frustrating, but a credit score can go down instead of up after someone pays off their car. That's mostly due to credit mix. If the car loan is the only installment loan the borrower has, then they'll have a less diverse credit mix once that loan is closed.

New Credit

New credit makes up 10% of your FICO Score. Applying for and receiving many cards and loans in a short period of time can be a red flag for a lender. In theory, a borrower who has a handle on their money shouldn't need to keep asking for new credit. New credit looks at how young your newest account is and how long it's been since you've applied for a card, loan, or line of credit.

FACTORS THAT DETERMINE A VANTAGESCORE

VantageScore's rating factors are similar to FICO's, but it reviews six factors instead of five. Like with FICO, payment history is the most important rating factor. In fact, it's a little more important with VantageScore, with 40% weight compared to FICO's 35%. The factors are broken out as seen in the following list:

- Payment history: 40%
- Depth of credit: 21%
- Credit utilization: 20%
- Balances: 11%
- Recent credit: 5%
- Available credit: 3%

Although VantageScore calls its factors by a different name, many mean just about the same thing as FICO's. VantageScore's depth of credit is the equivalent to FICO's length of credit history; credit utilization and balances are like amounts owed. Still, these nuances between VantageScore and FICO Score mean that borrowers usually have a slightly different VantageScore than a FICO Score—and it's likely that the VantageScore is higher. With available credit only making up 3% of the factors, VantageScore 4.0 puts less weight on how much credit a borrower has (ideal for those new to credit).

THE POWER OF TRENDED DATA

Another important distinction between FICO and VantageScore 4.0 is that the latter uses trended data to calculate a credit score. Some FICO Score models do too, such as FICO 10T (T stands for "trended"), but FICO 10T has yet to be adopted by most lenders. Trended data observes a borrower's behavior over a period of time, not just the borrower's standing at the time of application.

Borrowers chipping away at larger amounts of debt can benefit from trended data. A classic FICO Score doesn't look at trends and instead calculates your credit score based on a snapshot of your credit at the present time. As a result, classic FICO might penalize a borrower with more debt than a scoring model that uses trended data would—it depends on when the snapshot was taken.

Imagine this scenario: You've been carrying a $15,000 balance on a credit card for a year. You're determined to get the card paid off, so you've been paying a little more than the minimum amount due each month. Your payments are always on time, and you've cut your balance by more than half. You only have $8,000 of debt to go.

Your discipline with payments will be a boon, regardless of the credit scoring model. Payment history is the largest rating factor for both VantageScore and FICO. However, VantageScore 4.0

considers trends. It "sees" that you still have quite a bit of credit card debt to go, but that you've been making consistent payments that are above the minimum. Trended data predicts that you will continue this pattern and, in turn, your VantageScore 4.0 may get a boost. A classic FICO Score, on the other hand, won't use your past payment history for predictions. Instead, it takes a snapshot, and that snapshot reveals $8,000 in revolving credit card debt with no regard to how you may continue paying it off.

HARD AND SOFT CREDIT INQUIRIES

Will That Credit Check Hurt Your Score?

Lenders have two ways to check your credit score. They can use a soft credit inquiry, which helps them determine whether you meet their general eligibility guidelines before you officially apply. Or they can conduct a hard credit inquiry, which does impact your score. These give the lender access to your full credit report and indicate to other lenders that you applied for a loan, card, or other credit product.

That begs the question: Does a hard credit inquiry show the lender more information than a soft inquiry? Sometimes, but not always. Hard inquiries are standardized, but soft inquiries have different "levels." The type and breadth of information the lender sees through a soft credit check depends on the type of soft credit check it runs.

SOFT CREDIT INQUIRIES

A soft credit inquiry (also known as a soft credit hit, soft credit check, or soft credit pull) is an educational tool, and it does not impact a borrower's credit score. Lenders use soft credit inquiries to prescreen applicants. Landlords sometimes use it when reviewing prospective tenants. It's common for a utility company to conduct a soft credit pull to determine if it will require a deposit from a new customer. And when you check your credit score for free, what you see is based on a soft credit inquiry. Soft credit inquiries let you or whoever is doing the pulling take a pulse check on your credit without damaging scores.

A borrower doesn't need to give permission to a lender before it conducts a soft credit pull. This is what allows lenders to send out preapproved offers online or through the mail. Based on the information the lender can see with a soft credit inquiry, it has decided that you may be a good candidate for a credit product, and that triggers this type of advertising. Soft credit inquiries show basic financial information, such as the borrower's:

- Name, birthday, and current address
- Current credit lines, like credit cards and loans
- Credit score range
- Open bank accounts and recent overdrafts
- Payment history, including outstanding debts and missed payments reported by lenders
- Public records, such as bankruptcies

Soft pulls give access to parts of a borrower's credit report, but how much information is shown depends on the type of soft pull used. An account review inquiry includes the same information as a hard credit pull. Many lenders and credit card companies use these to periodically monitor their current borrowers and/or to preemptively offer credit limit increases. Other soft pulls are more limited in scope and simply help the lender confirm your identity or send potential borrowers preapproved offers. For the most part, only borrowers themselves can see soft credit hits on their credit report. How long borrowers can see soft inquiries on their credit report depends on the soft inquiry in question. Soft credit inquiries conducted for promotional prescreening only appear for one year, while account review inquiries can show for two. But remember— neither impact the borrower's credit score.

HARD CREDIT INQUIRIES

Hard credit inquiries do impact credit scores, but usually by five points or less (for FICO Scores). And although hard credit inquiries show on a credit report for two years, they typically only impact a credit score for one. Since hard hits impact credit scores, a borrower must give permission before inquiries can be conducted. A hard credit inquiry gives full access to a borrower's credit report. These inquiries include everything that is shown on a soft credit inquiry, plus additional details like:

- Credit utilization, or how much credit the borrower has compared to how much they have available to use
- Hard credit inquiries conducted over the last two years
- Length of credit history
- Number of new accounts

This broader information can help a lender better assess risk. After conditionally approving a borrower with a soft credit pull, the lender could change its mind once it conducts a hard credit inquiry. For instance, if a hard credit inquiry shows several hard credit pulls for other loan applications, the lender might deny the borrower. A series of hard credit hits over a short amount of time could be a sign that the borrower is scrambling for credit due to money mismanagement.

Rate Shopping Windows

Rate shopping windows protect credit by counting multiple hard credit hits as one for a certain period of time. This lets borrowers compare rates without taking too many credit dings. Window length depends on the credit scoring model the lender uses. Play it safe and get your shopping done within fourteen days, the shortest window of all the models.

THE DIFFERENCE BETWEEN PREQUALIFICATION AND PREAPPPROVAL

Many lenders use the terms "prequalification" and "preapproval" interchangeably, but these processes aren't the same. Prequalified is a prescreened offer based on a soft credit hit. Preapproval is a credit "quote" based on a hard credit inquiry, your credit report, and other documents. Preapprovals aren't guarantees, but they are as close as a borrower can get without actually signing a loan agreement.

PREQUALIFCATION VERSUS PREAPPROVAL		
TYPE OF APPROVAL	**PREQUALIFICATION**	**PREAPPROVAL**
What it is	A preliminary way to check eligibility and rates	A final step in the credit approval process
Why it's used	Used by borrowers to check eligibility; used by lenders for prescreened promotional offers	Used by borrowers during final shopping stages; used by lenders during the final application process
Type of credit inquiry	Soft credit inquiry	Hard credit inquiry
Credit impact	None	Shows on your report for 2 years; typically only affects score for 1 year
Information required	Self-reported personal and financial information	Confirmed personal and financial information through documents like IDs and pay stubs
Accuracy	Not very accurate; gives a borrower an idea whether they are eligible for the product	Highly accurate; as close to formal approval as a borrower can get

Chapter 3

Building Credit from Scratch

It can take just a month to generate a VantageScore, but a FICO Score can take six months. A consumer that hasn't generated a credit score is known to be "credit invisible." In the eyes of lenders, it's generally better to have no credit than it is to have bad credit. But that doesn't mean it'll be much easier to get a loan or card. Remember that credit is a system based on trust. If a consumer has yet to establish that trust through a history of on-time payments on several different types of credit lines, lenders are usually tight-fisted with their money.

So that brings us to the age-old catch-22: You need credit to build credit, but how do you build credit when lenders aren't willing to take a chance on you? It can be difficult, but it's not impossible. This chapter outlines steps consumers can take to build credit from scratch, including targeting credit products designed to build credit, enlisting the help of friends and family, and using tools that manually add nontraditional payments (like rent) to your credit report.

CREDIT-BUILDER LOANS

Loans That Work Backward to Build Payment History

Ultimately, it will take time and, in most cases, money, to build credit. But there are easier ways to do so than to apply for credit cards and loans that will likely be denied due to lack of credit. When used correctly, a credit-builder loan can be an effective way of building credit when you're starting from zero.

WHAT IS A CREDIT-BUILDER LOAN?

A credit-builder loan doesn't work like a traditional loan: Instead of *getting* money from the lender, the borrower *gives* money to the lender. You can think of this as a deposit. The lender puts this money into a locked savings account. Then, the borrower makes monthly payments to the lender to unlock the funds. The lender reports these payments to the credit bureaus, helping the borrower build payment history. Each lender decides exactly how its credit-builder loans are structured. With some, the borrower will get a little bit of their money back as they complete each monthly payment. With others, the borrower must "pay back" their loan in full before the lender will release any of the deposit.

Most credit-builder loans cost money, either through interest, monthly fees, or both. However, annual percentage rates (APRs; or yearly costs) are typically lower than average. For one, credit-builder loans are secured, and secured loans are almost always cheaper than unsecured. If you stop paying the lender, the lender gets to keep your deposit.

For lenders, credit-builder loans may be a way to earn repeat customers. If a borrower builds sufficient credit with a credit-builder loan, they might request a traditional loan or card with the same lender in the future. With this in mind, lenders tend to keep rates lower. Some even refund a portion of the interest the borrower paid at the end of the loan term, assuming the borrower made all of their payments on time.

Do Credit-Builder Loans Actually Work?

Credit-builder loans work best if you don't already have debt. According to a Consumer Financial Protection Bureau study, credit-builder loans increased the odds of generating a credit score by 24% if the borrower didn't have existing loans. Their scores also went up sixty points more on average compared to those who already had debt.

WHAT TO LOOK FOR

Credit-builder loans aren't the most common product, but they can be found with some banks, credit unions, and online fintech companies. A fintech company is an online platform that drives business to partner lenders. Generally, borrowers will find the best rates and terms with a credit union, but credit union membership is required. It can be easier and faster to get a credit-builder loan from a fintech company like Credit Karma and MoneyLion, but fintechs are more likely to charge fees for their services. When shopping for a credit-builder loan, there are several attributes to look for.

Low Rates
Credit-builder loans are an investment in your future, which means they can generally be considered good debt. That doesn't mean you should overpay for the privilege. Find a few lenders that offer credit-builder loans and note their APRs. The lower the APR, the less the loan will cost you in the long run.

Long Loan Terms
The point of a credit-builder loan is to create a positive payment history, so borrowers should choose a long repayment term. And unlike other types of loans, it's not ideal to pay off a credit-builder loan early. That defeats the purpose of the loan.

No Monthly Fees
Since credit-builder loans work best when you have them for a longer time, monthly fees can rack up. Imagine that your credit-builder loan has a twelve-month term and the fintech company charges a $19.99 monthly fee. If so, you'd have paid nearly $240 in fees alone over the year.

Interest Givebacks
Some lenders (mostly credit unions and banks) return some of the interest you paid when you pay off your credit-builder loan. This "reward" lowers the cost of the loan. However, the lender might charge higher interest rates to make up for this giveback, so borrowers should use a personal loan calculator (which can be easily found online) to see if the giveback actually works out in their favor.

Opportunities for Dividends

Some credit unions use the borrower's share account as collateral rather than asking for a separate deposit. A share account is the equivalent to a bank's savings account. Since credit unions are technically owned by their members, members earn a portion of the credit union's profit. This comes in the form of dividends. When credit unions use a share account for a credit-builder loan, that money sits locked in that share account where it can continue to earn dividends as the borrower pays their loan.

Whether a Deposit Is Required

A few credit-builder loans don't require a deposit. Instead, the borrower will make monthly payments (usually via autopay), and the lender will set the funds aside in a locked account. Once the credit-builder account reaches a certain amount, the lender releases the funds and considers the loan paid. This option can be good for borrowers who can't make the initial deposit needed for a traditional credit-builder loan.

SECURED CREDIT CARDS

A Starter Card with Guardrails

Applying for a credit card and getting denied due to a lack of credit history is frustrating, and to make things worse, it can leave your score a little worse off due to the hard credit hit. A secured credit card can be a great workaround for this process. Like credit-builder loans, secured cards are mainly used to generate or improve credit scores.

WHAT IS A SECURED CREDIT CARD?

A secured credit card is a credit card that requires a cash deposit, and that deposit serves as the card's credit line. For example, if a borrower makes a $200 deposit on a secured card, the card will have a $200 line of credit. According to the Consumer Finance Institute, there are about 3.7 million secured credit cards regularly used in America, equaling roughly $817 million in total debt. Even so, only about 2% of credit cards are secured.

Like standard credit cards, secured cards are revolving. The credit card issuer reports payments to the credit bureaus as the borrower charges and repays. If the borrower uses the card responsibly and makes their payments on time, the card issuer may eventually "graduate" the borrower to a standard, unsecured credit card and return their deposit. Before graduating, the credit card issuer will also consider other factors, like borrowers' credit utilization ratio and general credit health. Typically, credit-invisible borrowers usually graduate quicker than those who have low credit scores and/or other sources of debt.

It's Your Deposit. Spend It Wisely.

Credit-builder loans and secured cards yield similar results, but between the two, secured credit cards take more discipline to use. It can be easy to overspend when using a credit card, no matter the type. Credit interest also compounds. Carrying a balance from month to month can lead to runaway interest.

WHAT TO LOOK FOR IN A SECURED CREDIT CARD

Borrowers have more options when it comes to secured credit cards than they do with credit-builder loans. Virtually every major card issuer offers them, and each card comes with its own unique features, rates, and terms. When comparing cards, there are a few qualities that a prospective user should look out for.

Reporting to All Three Credit Bureaus

Since secured cards are designed to build credit, borrowers should make absolutely certain that the card they choose reports payments to all three credit bureaus. Some cards only report to one or two.

Deposit Amounts That Meet Financial Goals

Most major secured credit cards require an initial deposit of at least $200, and depending on the issuer, borrowers could put down as much as $5,000. The more a borrower uses and repays a secured credit card, the more payment history they'll accumulate. A larger deposit amount means more opportunities for credit growth, but also more opportunities to overspend. Finding this line is a balancing act, and it requires inward reflection. What deposit can you fit into your budget, and can you handle a larger credit line responsibly?

Clear Graduation Requirements

Typical graduation periods for most secured cards range from six months to a year or more. A graduation period is the length of time a cardholder must responsibly carry their secured card before the issuer will offer an unsecured credit card. Other than generating or improving a credit score, a secured card also teaches borrowers how to use credit responsibly by using their deposit as a guardrail. Borrowers shouldn't necessarily pick a card with the shortest graduation period, because that's less practice using the card. It's better to find a card that has a published graduation timeline that works for you.

For example, Bank A's card doesn't automatically review a cardholder for graduation for at least eighteen months. Bank B's card reviews graduation eligibility after just six months. If you want some extra time establishing healthier credit card habits, then Bank A's card is the better choice, since you have to wait at least a year and a half before graduating (unless you ask for a manual review). If you are looking to build credit fast, and you trust that you can avoid overspending once you qualify for an unsecured card, then Bank B's card might make more sense.

No Annual Fees

Most secured credit cards don't have an annual fee, but some do. Unless the card offers a major perk (like a super generous cashback bonus), borrowers who can qualify should prioritize no-fee cards.

Reward Possibilities

Secured cards frequently have some sort of rewards program as an extra benefit. Depending on the reward structure, borrowers can earn a percentage back every time they use their card. Sometimes, the cashback earned depends on the type of purchase. For example, groceries and gas might earn 2% cashback, but all other purchases might only earn 1%. Some cards have a flat cashback rate; while these can be easier to track, borrowers might end up with less earning potential. Usually, cashback rewards are applied as a statement credit, but they can also be sent to the borrower's checking account or be issued as a paper check or gift card.

Low Rates

Borrowers should always aim to get the lowest possible APR. But in an ideal world, credit card rates wouldn't be a concern, since it's best practice to pay off balances before the end of their billing cycle to avoid interest. Still, the lower the rate, the better, as you could have no choice but to carry a balance in a financial emergency.

BECOMING AN AUTHORIZED USER

Build Credit by Piggybacking

Credit piggybacking, or the act of becoming an authorized user on someone else's credit card, is a common way to generate a credit score and payment history. It doesn't require the user to apply for their own card or loan. Instead, the cardholder requests to add the authorized user to their already-established account. An authorized user can establish payment history, length of credit history, and amounts owed—FICO's most influential credit scoring factors—by credit piggybacking. Assuming this is the authorized user's first experience with a credit card, they will also be diversifying their credit mix, a smaller (yet still important) FICO factor.

WHAT IS AN AUTHORIZED USER?

An authorized user (or an authorized signer) is someone who has permission from a cardholder and their bank to use the cardholder's credit card. When an authorized user gets added, they "inherit" the card's payment and credit history, but the credit card account remains in the original cardholder's name. The authorized user also isn't responsible for any debt accrued on the card, even if they were the ones to rack it up.

There are no credit checks when someone requests to add an authorized user to their card. The bank isn't typically concerned with the authorized user's credit, since the debt remains the responsibility of the cardholder. That means limited or bad credit shouldn't be a hurdle for an authorized user. Still, it is possible for the bank to deny adding the authorized user if the user has a negative history with the bank, such as a past due balance or overdrawn account. Most banks and card issuers also require that an authorized user be a certain age, usually a minimum of thirteen to sixteen years old.

Be a Polite Guest

Before becoming an authorized user, establish some expectations with the cardholder. Do they want you to use the card at all, or are they simply doing you a favor by helping you build credit history? Having these conversations up front can prevent burned bridges in the future.

CHOOSING THE RIGHT CARDHOLDER

Just like a cardholder should be wary about who they add as an authorized user, those looking to piggyback need to be selective about who they ask for help. If the cardholder has missed a lot of payments or is at risk of future missed payment due to debt overload, getting added as an authorized user can hurt more than it helps. Remember that the card's history, whether good or bad, becomes the user's history too. Other than a long, positive payment history, authorized users should look for cardholders who have a high credit limit, healthy spending habits, and a mainstream bank card that they actually use.

High Credit Limit

By choosing a cardholder with a higher credit limit, the authorized user is better protected against a high credit utilization ratio. If the cardholder makes a big charge, say $5,000 on a card that has a $15,000 credit limit, the authorized user would be inheriting a credit utilization ratio of a little over 33% on that card. If it had a $50,000 spending limit, that ratio would drop to 10%. Generally, lenders do not look favorably on credit utilization ratios above 30%.

Healthy Spending Habits

If the cardholder habitually carries a balance from month to month, that could also impact the authorized user's credit utilization ratio. As interest accumulates, the credit card balance grows, and as a result, credit utilization goes up.

A Well-Used Mainstream Bank Card

Lenders usually view bank-issued credit cards in a better light than store cards, since mainstream credit cards are harder to qualify for. The cardholder should also use (and pay off) the card regularly. If the card sits idle, it won't do much for the authorized user.

AUTHORIZED USERS MAY STILL BE REJECTED

Credit piggybacking can be a great way to start building credit, but it might not be enough to qualify for your own loan or card. That's not because there's something wrong or immoral with credit piggybacking—it's a common personal finance strategy. But lenders can tell by looking at a credit report whether someone is an authorized user or a primary cardholder. Since authorized users aren't legally obligated to the debt, it doesn't help the lender assess the authorized user's risk. The authorized user hasn't yet proved that they can handle debt of their own. That means an authorized user could have an excellent credit score because of credit piggybacking but still end up denied when they apply by themselves. Being an authorized user also doesn't account for credit mix, a smaller credit scoring factor that can make or break the ability to borrow.

To illustrate this, let's consider the following scenario. An authorized user just started their credit journey last year by getting added to a loved one's card. They've been on the card for a year, and they now have a FICO Score of 780, firmly in the "very good" credit band. The authorized user hasn't applied for any new loans or cards since being added, but now they're ready to buy a car. They assumed that they'd have no trouble getting financed, but main-stream auto loan lenders turned them down. Why? Because they have no experience handling their own debt, let alone a car loan. Although credit mix only makes up 10% of a FICO Score, lenders might not be willing to take a chance on someone whose sole credit history is based on a single credit card, and as an authorized user at that. Lenders want to see that an applicant can juggle multiple types of credit while continuing to make on-time payments.

JOINT LOANS

Shared Loan, Shared Responsibilities

A joint loan has two borrowers rather than one. Each has equal access to the money or property obtained with the loan. Becoming a co-borrower on a joint loan might sound similar to becoming an authorized user on a credit card, but there's a huge distinction between the two: On a joint loan, both borrowers are equally liable for the debt, while an authorized user is not. Joint loans have a larger impact on credit scores as a result of this shared responsibility. This can be great if all payments are made on time, or it can backfire if one or both borrowers fall behind.

HOW JOINT LOANS WORK

A joint loan is a venture between two borrowers. In some situations, a loan could have more than two co-borrowers, but this is rare and usually only occurs with business loans. Co-borrowers don't have to be related, but they should at least have a friendly relationship. Both borrowers own the debt, so debt-to-income ratios are impacted for both people, and late or on-time payments affect both credit scores equally.

There are credit reporting codes that signify whether a loan is jointly owned. For instance, a jointly owned loan will show the code "Joint Account-Contractual Responsibility-2." That doesn't mean any one borrower is more responsible than the other; it only indicates to lenders that the loan is jointly owned. In contrast, the code for authorized users is "Joint Account-Authorized User-3." When a lender is reviewing a credit report, a borrower with a thin credit profile may benefit more from a joint loan than they would if they were an authorized user. That's because authorized users aren't responsible for the debt, but co-borrowers are.

Co-borrowers and Cosigners

A co-borrower has equal rights to the loan (or whatever the loan buys). They also are equally responsible for loan payments. Cosigners do not have rights to the loan, and they are only responsible for payments if the primary borrower defaults. Missed payments hurt both co-borrowers' and cosigners' credit.

TALKING TO YOUR CO-BORROWER BEFORE SIGNING

Open communication is key to successfully managing a joint loan. You may need to work with your co-borrower for many years, depending on how long your loan term is. It's essential for you and your co-borrower to have contingency plans before jumping into a joint loan.

Interest and Fees

If you're getting a joint loan only to build credit, you need to decide if the loan's interest and fees are worth it. Do you have a cheaper way to establish credit (such as a credit-builder loan), or are higher APRs (or yearly costs) worth it for quicker results? It's also not ideal to take on unnecessary debt, so be sure to have a good use for the loan outside of just building credit.

Sharing the Joint Loan

Some popular types of joint loans include auto loans, mortgages, and personal loans. Sharing an auto loan or mortgage can be straightforward when you're sharing the property with a spouse or loved one. But in the case of a personal loan, how will you share the funds? You could get a personal loan that can help you reach a shared goal. A wedding loan with your soon-to-be betrothed is one example. If you're only getting a joint personal loan for credit-building purposes, you'll both need to decide how to spend the money. Remember, a joint loan isn't split fifty-fifty. Both parties have equal, 100% access to the loan.

Handling Payments

Both borrowers are responsible for payments. Is your co-borrower going to send you their portion of the payment while you handle actually paying the lender? Or will both of you pay independently, perhaps via the lender's online portal? If one of you is collecting and making payments, what day of the month should the co-borrower send in their portion to ensure that the lender is paid on time? How will funds be transferred between borrowers—electronically, by paper check, or in cash?

Emergency Situations

If one borrower loses their job, gets sick, or otherwise can't make their part of the loan payment, can the other borrower pick up the slack? If this situation does occur, how will the borrower who has fallen behind catch up? These questions are especially important to answer so that contingency plans can be made quickly and not tank your credit scores.

A Faltering Relationship

No one goes into a joint loan assuming the relationship that they have with their co-borrower will fall apart, but sometimes life happens. Removing someone from a loan can be challenging. In almost all cases, the loan will need to be refinanced to remove someone's name. Refinancing can be expensive (or impossible) if you have a low credit score. You'll have to prove to the lender that you can handle the loan on your own merit, without the help of your co-borrower. Some loans have provisions that allow you to remove a cosigner, but these removal clauses aren't typical for joint loans.

USING RENT AND UTILITIES TO BOOST CREDIT

Get Credit for As Many On-Time Payments As Possible

Not every payment is reported to the credit bureaus, which may be good or bad based on the payment you're making. If you're late by a few days on your electricity bill, for example, you don't need to worry about a hit to your credit score. However, that also means that some of the first types of bills consumers are responsible for (related to their potential apartment's cost, for example) won't help them build credit.

TYPES OF PAYMENTS THAT DON'T BUILD CREDIT

If the bill isn't tied to a credit product like a loan or a credit card, the payment probably won't help the borrower build or improve their score. Some non-credit-building payments include:

- Rent
- Utilities (electricity, water, and gas)
- Car insurance
- Streaming subscriptions
- Internet and cell phone services

Late Payments Can Still Hurt

Paying bills on time won't impact a borrower's credit score unless the lender regularly sends data to a credit bureau, but very late payments can hurt. Companies may still report past due payments if they don't report on-time payments, especially if the bill is thirty or more days overdue.

GETTING CREDIT FOR NONTRADITIONAL PAYMENTS

It is possible to get nontraditional payments added to a credit report, but it doesn't happen automatically. The borrower must sign up for a service that manually reports these payments to the credit bureaus. There's a lot of variation in these types of services. Some have a "look back" period, where they will add payments the consumer has made over a certain period of time, like two years. Others only add payments from the point the consumer signed on. Sometimes these services are free, but often the consumer has to pay a monthly fee.

Behind the scenes, these companies aren't just reporting payments but adding new tradelines to the consumer's credit report. "Tradeline" is another word for an account. For instance, an installment loan (like an auto loan) shows as an installment tradeline. Once added, utility and other nontraditional payments appear as open tradelines on a credit report. That means these accounts don't have a specific credit limit, but payments are due in full each month (like rent). There are three main ways these services keep track of the payments you make:

- **Bank account monitoring:** Some services link directly to the consumer's bank account. Then, the service reports nontraditional payments as the consumer makes them, based on their bank account activity.
- **Utility account monitoring:** Other services require the consumer to hand over their online log-ins for the account they want credit for. These services monitor payment activity via the consumer's online portal.
- **Manual verification:** Rent reporting services often require that the consumer's landlord participate in the process. The service will confirm with the landlord that the consumer is indeed a tenant, and the landlord will also need to let the service know via text, phone call, or email that you made your payment.

WHEN CONSIDERING A PAYMENT REPORTING SERVICE

Utility and rent reporting can help credit-limited borrowers build a score, but these services do have some drawbacks. From requiring private information to charging fees that are simply not worth it, you have to be careful as you research for a payment reporting service.

Some Require Sensitive Information

Consumers might not feel comfortable linking bank accounts or handing over online log-in information. If someone is considering signing up for a service, they should make sure the company they choose is reputable. Trustpilot reviews are a good place to start. The Consumer Financial Protection Bureau also maintains a database of customer complaints it receives against financial institutions; you can check the site at www.consumerfinance.gov/data-research/consumer-complaints.

Only Report to One Bureau

Few, if any, services send payment information to all three bureaus. If the service is owned by a bureau (such as Experian Boost or TransUnion's TruVision Resident Credit), then that service probably only affects that specific credit bureau. So, take a close look, as your credit across all three bureaus is important.

Reported Payments Won't Affect All Credit Scoring Models

Some newer credit scoring models (such as FICO 10T and VantageScore 4.0) already incorporate rent payments. But older models (like FICO Scores 5, 4, and 2) do not, regardless of whether the consumer enrolls in a rent reporting service. If a consumer is trying to improve their score for a specific model, they should double check that the type of payments the service reports will impact that model.

Expensive Fees

Depending on the service, a consumer may only see a small increase in their score, if they see one at all. Free, legitimate payment reporting services may be worth a shot, but some cost hundreds in monthly subscription fees. It may be better to take that money and use it as a deposit on a secured credit card or credit-builder loan.

Cancelling the Service May Mean a Closed Tradeline

Most payment reporting services close whatever tradeline they opened on a credit report if the consumer cancels their subscription. Closed accounts can still help a borrower's credit score, as closed accounts that were paid on time show on a credit report for up to ten years. However, the consumer's credit score may be negatively affected when the service closes the tradeline, as this impacts the consumer's length of credit history, which makes up 15% of a FICO Score.

Chapter 4

Common Credit Pitfalls

There's a common saying, "if only I knew then what I know now." Life is full of mistakes, and some are easier to bounce back from than others. Seemingly small credit gaffes may have harsher consequences than you'd expect. Late payments, for example, typically appear on your credit report for seven years. Just one bill that fell through the cracks can follow you for nearly a decade.

Not all credit pitfalls are due to falling behind or taking on more debt than you can chew, however. Some are a result of good intentions, like cosigning on a loan. Unfortunately, credit bureaus don't consider intent. And unless an adverse mark is due to a credit reporting error, there are few do-overs when a borrower makes a mistake that harms their score. The best way to free yourself from financial regret is to avoid mistakes in the first place. This chapter takes you through the more common potential problems when it comes to credit, from consistently paying late to taking on predatory loans.

THE LATE PAYMENT LIFE CYCLE

Behind the Scenes of a Late Payment

Payment history is the most significant credit scoring factor for both FICO Score and VantageScore, so it's worth examining exactly what happens when a borrower misses a due date. Some may get lucky and avoid a hit to their credit score if they pay within their grace period (if their lender offers one). If the borrower falls too far behind, not only will their score drop, but they could also put themselves at risk for a lawsuit.

THE TIMELINE OF EVENTS ON DELINQUENT PAYMENTS

Technically, a payment is late (or delinquent) as soon as the borrower misses their due date, even by just one day. That doesn't mean that the lender is going to report the late payment to the credit bureaus right away. However, if the bill remains unpaid for an extended period, the lender could consider the loan to be in default. When this happens, the lender stops trying to collect payment and sells the debt to a debt collection agency. Each lender decides whether it will provide a grace period and, if so, how long it is. It's important that borrowers check their loan or credit card agreements to see exactly how their lender handles late payments. Still, in the following table, you'll find some general guidelines.

LATE PAYMENT TIMELINE			
TYPE OF LOAN	TYPICAL GRACE PERIOD BEFORE FEES	DAYS UNTIL PAYMENT IS REPORTED	DAYS UNTIL LOAN IS IN DEFAULT
Mortgage	10 to 15 days	30 days	90 to 120 days
Auto loan	10 to 15 days	30 days	30 to 90 days
Credit card	21 to 25 days	30 to 60 days	180 days
Personal loan	10 to 15 days	30 days	90 to 120 days
Federal student loan	180 to 270 days	90 days	270 days

Paid Within the Grace Period

As long as the borrower pays by the end of their grace period (when applicable), the lender should not charge a late fee, and the late payment won't affect the borrower's credit score. If the borrower misses their grace period, the lender may charge a late fee. Late fees vary by lender or type of loan. Fees for late credit card payments are regulated by the Credit Card Accountability Responsibility and Disclosure (CARD) Act of 2009.

Currently, credit card issuers can charge up to $30 on a first late payment and $41 for late payments after that. For a brief moment in 2024, these fees were reduced to $8, but these changes were reversed in 2025. Although personal loans are regulated by their own acts and laws (Truth in Lending Act, Military Lending Act, Equal Credit Opportunity Act, and state usury laws), there are no such caps on late payments.

Lender Reports Late Payment(s) to Credit Bureaus

A late payment can drop a credit score by as much as one hundred points, depending on the borrower's credit score and the credit scoring model. Generally, a late payment causes a larger drop for a higher credit score than for a lower score. When a good or excellent credit borrower pays late, lenders usually consider this a harbinger of more repayment problems. This significantly raises the risk for that borrower, which is then reflected in that borrower's score.

Being Issued a Penalty APR

A lender could increase a borrower's rate if they fall far enough behind. This is called a penalty annual percentage rate (APR; or yearly costs). The CARD Act allows credit card companies to raise existing APRs after a borrower is sixty days late. Penalty APRs can sometimes be as high as 29.99%. If the borrower doesn't get caught up soon, their debt burden will begin to skyrocket. Personal loan lenders also often charge penalty APRs, but it's up to the company and the borrower's state usury laws to decide when penalty APRs apply.

Lender Continues to Attempt to Collect the Debt

As time goes on, the lender will become more persistent about getting paid. Snail mail, emails, text reminders, and phone calls may increase.

Lender Sells Debt to a Collection Agency

Once a borrower is late enough, the lender may charge off the debt. This means that the lender has given up on collecting the debt and has written it off as a business loss. After this, the lender could (and frequently will) sell the debt to a debt collection agency. Debt collection agencies pay very little for past due debt, but it depends on the age and type of debt.

Debt Collection Agency Attempts Collecting Debt

Compared to lenders, debt collection agencies can be quite aggressive in their collection efforts. Calls will ramp up, both to you and to friends, family, and your employer if the debt collector can't get ahold of you. There are rules on what debt collectors can and can't do, which we will cover later.

If the debt collection agency successfully collects the debt, the lender typically pays 25–50% of what the agency collected. This means the lender will recover some of its losses, and the debt collection agency will get a slice of the pie.

Debt Collection Agency Issues a Lawsuit

If the borrower doesn't pay the debt collector, the debt collector may sue the borrower. Debt collection lawsuits start with a court summons. If the borrower fails to respond to the summons, the court may issue a money judgement against them. A money judgement allows the debt collection agency to take more serious measures in recovering what is owed. This could include wage garnishment and bank account levies, which would allow the collector to freeze and withdraw money from the borrower's bank account.

Secured Loans and Repossession

A lender will repossess collateral if the borrower defaults, but some rules apply. Many states require auto loan lenders to give the borrower time to "cure the debt" (or get caught up) before they can repossess a car. Mortgage lenders, however, typically need to wait 120 days before initiating the foreclosure process.

PREDATORY LENDING

Easy to Borrow, Easy to Get Trapped

Predatory loans are designed to keep borrowers stuck in financial quicksand with high interest, expensive fees, and impossible due dates. In general, financial experts agree that a loan may be considered predatory if it carries an APR of 36% or higher, which is why many online lenders cap their rates to 35.99%. Unless you're in a dire situation and have exhausted every option available, avoid the following loans types throughout this entry, as they are generally considered predatory.

Get It in Writing

Borrowing from a loved one may be a better option than a high-interest loan. If you do borrow from a loved one, create a loan agreement (or promissory note) for the safety of all parties. A loan agreement will spell out the terms of the loan, like due dates and the loan's interest rate.

PAYDAY LOANS

A payday loan is a small-dollar loan that typically ranges from a few hundred dollars up to a thousand. Generally, payday loans work like this:

1. The borrower requests a loan from a payday lender. Some payday lenders have brick-and-mortar locations. Many operate entirely online.
2. Instead of conducting a hard credit check, the payday lender reviews how much the borrower gets paid and when. This is what the lender will use to determine the size of the loan and its due date.
3. The borrower must agree to pay the loan in full the next time they get paid. The payday lender may demand a post-dated check that lines up with the borrower's payday, but usually it requires an automatic withdrawal.

On paper, that doesn't sound so bad. A payday loan can seem like a quick way to bridge the gap for borrowers who are running short. It's true; they can be. However, payday loans have astronomical fees that can equate to APRs around 400%. While the annualized nature of APRs makes payday loans sound very expensive (and they are), APRs aren't necessarily the most accurate way to price a payday loan, as the loan is due in full in weeks to a month, not a year. It's the extremely short repayment terms and loan rollover options in addition to high fees that get borrowers locked in the payday loan loop.

Many states have usury (or lending) laws that restrict or prohibit payday loans. But depending on where the borrower lives, payday loans can come with fees between $10 and $30 for every $100 borrowed, according to the Consumer Financial Protection Bureau. ($15 for every $100 borrowed is common.) This is the equivalent of a 400% APR on a two-week loan. In this scenario, the borrower will owe $60 in fees on a $400 loan. If the borrower has that money come payday, then the payday loan was expensive but hopefully worth it to get by. But what happens if the borrower can't pay? Enter payday loan rollovers.

Payday Loan Rollovers

A payday loan rollover allows a borrower to take out another payday loan to cover their first. This is where a lot of borrowers get into trouble. Although the borrower gets extra time to pay, fees continue to rack up including those for the second loan, plus any financing charges the payday lender may levy for the rollover itself.

TRIBAL LOANS

Tribal loans are high-interest installment loans that are offered by Native American tribes and financed through third-party tribal lending entities, or TLEs. TLEs are considered an arm of the Native American tribe. Because of tribal sovereignty, state usury laws typically don't apply to tribal loans, and there are no nationwide federal usury laws. As a result, tribal loans can come with APRs even higher than payday loans, sometimes close to 1,000%.

Unlike payday loans, tribal loans generally have longer repayment terms, usually up to twenty-four months. At first glance, this can be a good thing. A borrower doesn't have to come up with a big chunk of change by their next due date. However, the longer it takes to pay off a loan, the more interest that will accumulate. With APRs in the triple and quadruple digits, that interest is substantial and means it will be a long time before the borrower starts chipping away at their principal.

BUY HERE, PAY HERE CAR LOANS

No credit, no problem! That's the mantra for buy here, pay here (BHPH) loans. A BHPH car lot is a dealership that finances the cars that it sells. That doesn't mean that every time a dealer helps a borrower get a car loan they're working with a BHPH loan. Most dealerships have a network of lenders that they have an incentive to work with. Instead, a BHPH lot provides the funding from its own coffers rather than being a conduit between car buyer and a lender or financial institution.

The car lot is acting as its own bank, so it gets to make up its own eligibility requirements, and these requirements are loose. BHPH dealerships target subprime borrowers, and as a result, a credit check isn't typically required. Instead, the borrower may be required to show proof of income through pay stubs and provide personal references. That makes these loans very risky for the dealership. To mitigate this risk, BHPH loans are very expensive, sometimes with APRs as high as 20%, according to Experian. Payments can be due weekly or biweekly rather than monthly, which gives the borrower more opportunity to fall behind. Knowing this, some BHPH car lots install GPS tracking in their cars to make repossession easier if the borrower can no longer pay.

Unlike other types of car loans, a BHPH loan doesn't usually help the borrower build credit. This is a huge disadvantage since the borrower probably has bad credit, and on-time car loan payments can be a huge credit score boost. However, the car lot will likely report late payments, repossessions, and how much has been sent to collections if it does repossess the car. When possible, borrowers should avoid loans that can't help build credit but still have the potential to hurt it.

Car Title Loans

A car title loan is a small-dollar, short-term loan that uses a car as collateral. Some non-predatory personal loans use cars as collateral, too, but car title loans are different. Instead of getting years to pay off the loan, the borrower typically has thirty days or less. Finance fees on car title loans are very high, sometimes equating to a triple-digit APR. If the borrower can't pay the loan back, they may have to roll the loan over into another one (much like a payday loan) to avoid losing their car to repossession.

MISMANAGEMENT OF HIGHER-RISK FINANCIAL TOOLS

Handle with Care

The types of loans listed throughout this entry aren't inherently "bad," but they do tend to cause problems if the borrower is not careful. Some of these options are so easy to use that the borrower ends up spending more than they can afford. Not only is this detrimental to your budget in the short term, but impulse shopping can hold you back from starting an emergency fund or investing for retirement. Other loans in this entry require collateral—very important collateral, like the borrower's home or car.

PAYCHECK ADVANCE APPS

A paycheck advance app allows workers to borrow from their paycheck before payday. At least, that's how these apps advertise themselves. Most often, though, they work more like payday loans. Most apps don't actually take the advance out of the borrower's paycheck. They instead require the borrower to repay on their payday, via automatic payments (not unlike payday loans).

Paycheck advance apps use a soft credit check and proof of income (usually by electronically connecting to the borrower's bank account and reviewing the cadence at which they get paid) to determine eligibility. These apps don't typically charge interest, but most come with fees. Monthly subscription fees, a flat fee for borrowing, fees for expedited advances, and optional tips aren't uncommon. Loan amounts usually start off low, maybe $20–$50. As the borrower demonstrates responsible use, the app may be willing to bump up loan amounts to several hundred dollars or more.

Paycheck advance apps can be helpful in an emergency, but they can also reinforce poor spending habits. Regularly needing money before payday can be a sign that the borrower is living above their means, needs a better budget, or should try for a higher-paying job. Some borrowers resort to downloading and cycling through multiple apps. Even though most loans through paycheck advance apps are small dollar amounts, they can add up when you have more than one loan out at a time.

What Is Earned Wage Access?

Some paycheck advance apps work on the earned wage access (EWA) model. EWA is generally considered to be more consumer-friendly than standard advances. With EWA, workers borrow from wages they've already earned. This guarantees loan payback, but because some EWAs automatically deduct loans from the borrower's paycheck, this could lead to a surprise come payday.

BUY NOW, PAY LATER

Buy now, pay later (BNPL) helps consumers break up retail purchases into more manageable payments. The most common payment plan is Pay in 4. With this, the borrower will pay 25% of the purchase at the time of sale. Then, the balance is due in three payments, each due every two weeks. Most apps offer other options, like Pay in 30.

No down payment is required for these loans, but the full purchase amount will be due in thirty days. Others offer longer-term financing akin to a personal loan, with repayment terms that can range from twelve to twenty-four months. It's easy to qualify for BNPL. Usually, eligibility is determined solely by a soft credit check, making them more accessible to borrowers with lower scores.

BNPL isn't necessarily a bad product. Unless the borrower chooses longer-term financing, most BNPL payment plans are interest-free. Some may also be fee-free if all payments are made on time. However, BNPL is also incredibly easy to use, and this could lead to impulse spending. Psychologically, buying clothes or other items that you want but don't actually need might not seem that big of a deal since you don't have to pay for them in full. Also, a borrower could find themselves juggling multiple due dates if they have more than one BNPL loan out at a time (maybe even through different apps). Due dates won't line up since they are based on the date of the purchase (unlike a credit card). BNPL requires automatic payments, so multiple BNPL loans could mean multiple BNPL payments a week, increasing the risk of overdrafts and budget shortages.

HOME EQUITY LOANS AND HELOCS

Home equity loans and home equity lines of credit (HELOCs) can be a great way for homeowners to borrow money, as long as there's a rock-solid payoff plan. These loans use the borrower's home as collateral, which can help the borrower pay a lower rate. But if something were to happen and the borrower could no longer make payments, their lender could foreclose on their home. That's not to mention the extra challenge of paying both a primary mortgage and the home equity loan or HELOC, assuming the borrower is still paying off their home.

VEHICLE-BACKED PERSONAL LOANS

Like home equity loans and HELOCs, vehicle-backed personal loans can be beneficial for the borrower. Offering collateral typically results in lower rates. However, the lender can repossess the borrower's car if they can't make their personal loan payments, causing a terrible domino effect. If a borrower's car is repossessed, then they may have a hard time getting to work. If the borrower has a hard time getting to work, they could lose their job or their employer might cut their hours. This will make it much more difficult for the borrower to work their way out of the hole and get another ride by either buying back their car or getting another car. (A car loan will probably be out of the question for quite some time due to the recent repossession.)

VEHICLE EQUITY LOANS

A vehicle equity loan is a little like a vehicle-backed personal loan. It allows borrowers to take a loan from the equity they have in their car. You can think of it almost like a second mortgage, but for car loans. Vehicle equity loans aren't a terrible idea for those in a pinch—they tend to have lower rates than unsecured personal loans since collateral is involved. But because collateral is involved, vehicle equity loans are higher risk. The lender will repossess the borrower's car if they don't pay back their loan.

SIMPLE MISTAKES THAT CAN SABOTAGE CREDIT

Little Blunders, Big Consequences

Once you learn what goes into a credit score (like you find in Chapter 2's entry "How Credit Scores Are Calculated"), it's easy to see how late payments and overapplying for credit cards can hurt you. Payment history accounts for 35% of a FICO Score, with new credit making up 10%. But in this entry, you'll find that there are also some everyday actions that can cause you to unintentionally hurt your score.

REFUSING TO TAKE OUT CREDIT

It's a good thing to be cautious with credit, but ignoring it to live a cash-only lifestyle isn't usually the answer. Credit and debt are nuanced. If a borrower with challenged credit decides to cut up their cards and tackle their debt, moving away from credit may be a great idea. However, if someone has the means to use credit without damaging their score, they might want to do that. Building a solid credit history grants access to large amounts of money in case of emergency. Also, avoiding credit could leave thousands of dollars on the table in the form of cashback, miles, and other rewards.

COSIGNING ON A CAR LOAN AS A FAVOR

You might be compelled to help a friend or family member by cosigning on a car loan. It's not always a bad move, but cosigning on a loan doesn't just mean that you're vouching for the borrower as a personal reference. You are equally responsible for payments. If you have any doubt that the potential car buyer can't keep up with the loan, don't cosign. The same goes if you can't afford to take over payments in an emergency.

If you still want to assist, consider becoming a co-borrower instead. The loan—and importantly, the car title—will be in your name as well as your loved one's. This gives you equal rights to the car. Cosigners don't get legal access to the car, even if they're on the hook for payments.

Consider the Insurance Implications

If you co-borrow with another person, you will likely need to be added to that person's car insurance policy. However, this shouldn't impact premiums if you have your own insurance. If you don't, you may be required to be added as an active driver.

USING A CREDIT CARD WITHOUT A SOLID PLAN

In a perfect world, borrowers should use a credit card in the same way that they would use their debit card. That is to say, if a borrower doesn't have enough money in their bank account to cover what they are putting on their credit card, they should not use a credit card and assume they'll have the funds when the bill rolls in. It's easy to get into the habit of using a credit card for quick coffee stops and other small purchases. These charges add up. Credit cards should be used for convenience and rewards only. The key to using a credit card to your advantage is to pay off the total balance by your statement date.

TAKING OUT A HIGHER-INTEREST LOAN ON A LOWER-VALUE CAR

Taking out an expensive loan on an older car puts the car buyer at risk for an upside-down car loan. When a borrower is upside-down, they owe more on the loan than what the property is worth.

Imagine this: A borrower with a 580 FICO Score buys a car with a loan at 15% APR. The car is seven years old. Kelley Blue Book values the car at $8,000, but the loan amount is $9,500. The dealer charged fees to process documents and talked the buyer into a dent and ding package. These expenses were rolled into the car loan. From the first day of ownership, the car buyer is already $1,500 underwater. As time goes on, the car will continue to depreciate.

In the meantime, the borrower continues to make car loan payments on time and in full, but interest is front-loaded on a car loan. At first, most of the borrower's car payment goes toward interest, not principal. Principal will go down slowly as the borrower continues to chip away at the loan, but as they do so, the car will continue to depreciate (especially if it starts to have mechanical troubles as an older model).

CARRYING A CREDIT CARD BALANCE

There's a misconception that carrying a credit card balance and making minimum payments is a strategy to boost credit utilization. This is a surefire way to pay unnecessary interest. The key is to use your credit card responsibly, regularly, and with intention, and to pay your balance off in full at each billing cycle. This'll help you establish a positive payment history while skipping interest altogether.

OPENING A STORE CARD YOU'LL RARELY USE

"Would you like to apply for a store card for an extra 15% off on today's purchase?" is a common saying at just about every department (and online) store these days. The extra savings are no doubt tempting, but unless you shop at that store frequently, the one-day discount probably isn't worth it.

When a borrower opens a store card, it will appear as new credit on their credit report. Not only that, but their credit utilization could skyrocket if the borrower makes a large initial purchase with said store card. And if the borrower doesn't use it often, the card issuer might deactivate it. Synchrony Bank, for example, is a prolific issuer of store cards, and it usually deactivates a card after a year or two of dormancy.

There is no standard timeframe for when a card issuer considers a card inactive, and there are no laws that state the card issuer must warn the cardholder that it will be deactivating the card soon. That decision is up to the issuer, so it's important for cardholders to check their contracts. In any case, closing a credit card account can negatively impact a borrower's credit utilization, age of accounts, and credit mix (if it's the borrower's only credit card).

THE DANGERS OF DEBT SETTLEMENT COMPANIES

Is the Savings Potential Worth the Risk?

When a borrower is overwhelmed with debt, they can call their lender or card issuer to see if they'd be willing to accept a smaller amount than what is actually due to close out the account. Or the borrower could pay a debt settlement company to negotiate on their behalf. Although credit score damage may be the same regardless of how the debt is settled, debt settlement companies can charge hefty fees. This entry breaks down how debt settlement programs work and the risks that accompany enrollment.

WHAT IS DEBT SETTLEMENT?

Debt settlement is a process in which a borrower negotiates the amount of unsecured debt they owe, such as credit cards, medical bills, and personal loans. The goal is to get lenders—and more often, debt collection agencies—to accept less than the total amount due and forgive the remaining balance.

The idea behind settlement is that a lender would rather get paid something than nothing at all. If a borrower is at the point of settling, they are usually far past due dates and may be in default. Debt collection agencies buy debt for much less than the debt is worth. When a debt collection agency is successful, the lender splits the collection proceeds with the collection agency, allowing it to recoup some of its losses. According to JG Wentworth, debts that are less than six months old may sell for seven to fifteen cents for every dollar owed. Credit card debt typically sells for four to seven cents, medical debt for one to five cents, and mortgage debt for two to five cents.

HOW A DEBT SETTLEMENT PROGRAM WORKS

Debt settlement can help borrowers pay less than what they owe, but there are some risks attached—namely, if the borrower decides to work with a debt settlement company. Other than bankruptcy, enrolling in a debt settlement program is the most drastic financial step that a borrower can take. The process looks like this:

1. The borrower finds a debt settlement company and enrolls in a program.
2. The debt settlement company opens an escrow account for the borrower, which may require a one-time start-up fee and monthly maintenance fees. An escrow account is a dedicated bank account that the borrower will use to save up money to use during negotiations. The borrower has full control over this account and can deposit and withdraw at will.
3. The debt settlement company instructs the borrower to quit paying their credit cards, personal loans, medical bills, and other eligible unsecured debt. The borrower will instead make monthly payments to the settlement company, and the company will put the money into the escrow account.

4. The borrower continues to make payments into the escrow account for twenty-four to forty-eight months, depending on the length of the debt settlement program and/or how fast the borrower can save.
5. Once enough funds are built in the escrow account, the debt settlement company will begin negotiating with creditors. If a settlement is successful, the creditor will accept less than what the borrower owes, and the debt settlement company will charge the borrower a fee of 15–25% of the amount of debt enrolled.

This sounds like a really great outcome, right? Well, it can be, when every piece comes together seamlessly, but there are potential risks.

THE RISKS OF DEBT SETTLEMENT PROGRAMS

Debt settlement might be a viable option for borrowers who have no hope of getting out of credit card debt but aren't ready to file for bankruptcy. Even so, it's generally seen as a high-risk, less-than-ideal solution by most financial experts. When working with a debt settlement company goes wrong, the borrower may find themselves worse off than before they enrolled.

Ruined Credit
The mechanism behind debt settlement requires borrowers to stop paying bills. This allows the borrower to save up money that the settlement company will use to negotiate. Most people who

enroll in debt settlement are already behind, but many programs take more than a year to complete. This extended barrage of late payments will tank the borrower's score. Furthermore, settled debt shows on credit reports for up to seven years. This will indirectly hurt the borrower's ability to borrow in the future, even if debt settlement itself isn't a credit scoring factor.

Ballooning Debt and High Fees

Borrowers could still pay up to 85% of what they owe even when a settlement is successful. Debt settlement companies charge settlement and escrow fees. Importantly, enrolling in a settlement program does not stop interest and late fees from accumulating on your credit cards.

Remember that credit card interest compounds daily. When you carry a balance from month to month, the issuer calculates how much interest you owe on your current balance that day. Then, it adds that interest to your total balance. Interest grows as bills go unpaid, and sometimes this accumulated interest can outweigh the money the borrower saved by settling.

Debt Settlement Scams Are Prevalent

In 2010, the Federal Trade Commission (FTC) amended the Telemarketing Sales Rule (TSR) to help protect consumers from shady debt settlement companies. Also called the Debt Relief Services Rule, this amendment banned debt relief companies from charging settlement fees before a debt is actually settled. Even so, debt settlement scams can be common, especially during times of economic uncertainty. Other than up-front fees, borrowers should avoid debt relief companies that:

- Claim to work for a government-backed debt relief program
- Don't clearly explain their fee structure or the risks associated with debt relief
- Make cold calls
- Overpromise or guarantee specific results

Any of these signs should sound the alarm to you that they are not looking out for your best interests.

Successful Settlement Isn't Guaranteed

Not all creditors are willing to negotiate. Ideally, a debt relief company should know which credit card issuers are more willing to play ball and which are not. American Express, for example, is notorious for its unwillingness to settle easily, if at all. The success of debt settlement also depends on what "stage" the debt is in. Collection agencies are typically more willing to settle than the creditor itself. In any case, if the creditor or collection agency isn't willing to settle, then the borrower stopped making payments and potentially ruined their credit score for zero results.

Settled Debt Is Taxable

The Internal Revenue Service (IRS) typically considers settled debt above $600 as regular income. When debt settlement does work, the borrower could face a hefty bill come tax time.

High Dropout Rate

Borrowers who enroll in debt settlement programs are unable to keep up with their credit card bills. But debt settlement still requires the borrower to make regular contributions to their escrow account so the settlement company has something to negotiate with. Past investigations conducted by the FTC and various state departments have shown that the average debt settlement program completion rate is less than 10%. Consumers are well within their rights to drop out early, but that does mean that they may have missed debt payments and accumulated interest for no reason.

Debt Lawsuits and Wage Garnishments

Enrolling in a debt settlement program won't stop a creditor or debt collection agency from suing. In fact, some debt settlement companies offer legal services if their client gets sued. Sometimes these services are included as part of enrollment, and sometimes the company charges for them à la carte. If the borrower ignores or loses the debt collection lawsuit, the court may issue a money judgement against them. This will allow the creditor or agency to garnish wages, freeze and seize bank accounts, and/or place liens on property.

THE TRUTH ABOUT CREDIT REPAIR COMPANIES

Worth the Cost or Better to DIY?

Consumer Reports once conducted a study to learn more about the frequency of credit reporting errors. The results were astonishing:

- 44% of the roughly 3,200 people who participated found an error on their credit report.
- 27% of those errors were severe enough that they had the potential to impact the borrower's credit score.
- 4,300 people volunteered to be a part of the survey, but only 3,200 could participate. The remaining 1,100 were not able to access their credit report.

Credit reporting errors are more common than many think. Some of these errors are administrative. While not ideal, a small mistake like that might not have an impact on credit scores. But what happens when the errors are more serious? It's one thing if the borrower's credit report lists an outdated address. It's something else if their report shows a delinquent bill although it's already been paid.

If you've found an error on your credit report, there are two paths you can take: Dispute the error yourself or hire a credit repair company to handle the problem for you. Credit repair companies review your credit report for errors and dispute them on your behalf. These services sound promising, but is the price tag worth it?

WHAT DOES A CREDIT REPAIR COMPANY DO?

Credit repair companies start by ordering your credit reports from one or more of the three bureaus (Equifax, Experian, and TransUnion). Then, they review the reports line by line and take note of any errors. If they find an error, they will dispute it on your behalf.

There's no guarantee that the dispute will lead to a change in your credit score or report, but the same goes if you dispute the error yourself. However, a credit repair company can make it easier for the borrower by offering a type of "white glove" service. The borrower hands over their personal information so the company can pull credit reports, and the company takes care of the rest.

THE COSTS OF CREDIT REPAIR

Credit repair services aren't cheap. Although pricing varies by company, consumers can expect to pay $50 to $150 a month until the process is complete (or until the consumer drops out of the program). More expensive plans can come with extra benefits, such as credit and identity theft monitoring. Credit repair companies frequently market their service as an investment, but in truth, they don't do anything that a consumer can't do on their own. Legitimate credit repair services can save consumers time and hassle, but the question is whether the cost is worth it.

According to major credit repair company Lexington Law, clients who saw an increase in their credit scores had an average boost of about forty points over six months' time. Although a forty-point increase isn't anything to sneeze at, results aren't guaranteed, and there may be cheaper, more effective ways of boosting credit (like disputing errors yourself or getting a secured credit card).

SIGNS OF A CREDIT REPAIR SCAM

In 2024, the Consumer Financial Protection Bureau found that Lexington Law illegally charged up-front fees for credit repair services. The CFPB also reported that Lexington engaged in bait-and-switch activities. As a result, Lexington Law was ordered to pay back billions in restitution and was banned from telemarketing credit repair services for ten years.

There are two main sets of laws that protect consumers from predatory credit repair practices: the Telemarketing Sales Rule of 1995 and the Credit Repair Organizations Act (CROA), passed in 1996. Consumers considering credit repair should familiarize themselves with the basic protections these laws provide to avoid getting duped by a sham company.

Charging a Fee Before Delivering Results

Credit repair companies are not allowed to charge any fees before they actually perform a service. They can, however, charge monthly subscription fees. The logic is that the monthly fee is for actions the company made in that month.

Offering to Create a New Credit Profile for You

Some scam credit repair services promise to wipe the slate clean by offering the consumer a brand-new credit report. To do this, the company will create a new identity for the consumer with a real Social Security number obtained through the dark web or other fraudulent means. This is called synthetic identity theft, and it's illegal.

Paying for Tradelines

Some companies may offer to sell you a tradeline, or account, to help build or improve your credit score. What you're actually doing is paying to become an authorized user on a stranger's credit card. Although not technically illegal, credit card issuers view buying tradelines as misrepresentation. Paying for tradelines is unethical at best and an identity theft risk at worst.

Promising to Remove Legitimate Derogatory Marks

Credit repair companies cannot promise to or attempt to remove legitimate derogatory marks on your credit report, such as late payments, debt settlements, or bankruptcy filings. Credit repair companies are also not allowed to advise consumers to dispute truthful information on their credit report.

Instructing to Avoid Contacting the Credit Bureaus/ Your Creditors

Consumers can order credit reports once a week for free. If the consumer finds an error, it is their legal right to dispute that error. Any company that tells a consumer that they should not order credit reports or dissuades a borrower from talking to their creditors may be dabbling in illegal activities.

Asking to Apply for an Unnecessary EIN

Employer identification numbers (EINs) are issued by the Internal Revenue Service (IRS), and they're almost like a Social Security number, but for businesses. The IRS uses a business's EIN for tax reporting. Scam credit repair companies sometimes direct clients to request an EIN through the IRS and to use this EIN in place of their Social Security number on loan and credit card applications. This is illegal.

Refusing to Provide Written Disclosures

The CROA mandates that all credit repair services provide written disclosures that inform consumers of their rights, including the right to dispute credit reporting errors themselves, for free. Disclosures must also advise consumers that they have the right to get their money back if they cancel their credit repair contract within three days of signing.

Asking to Be Paid with a Nontraditional Method

Fraudulent credit repair companies often demand payment via gift cards, cryptocurrency, money order, or by wire. That's because it's nearly impossible for a consumer to get their money back once they realize they've fallen victim to a scam.

Chapter 5

Fixing Credit Mistakes

Warren Buffett famously said that it takes twenty years to build a reputation and five minutes to ruin it. Credit can be the same way. Just one simple mistake, like a missed payment, could send a credit score tumbling. It's a good thing that there are proven strategies to counteract and fix these mistakes.

As you learn how to deploy these strategies, don't let perfect become the enemy of good. Of course, the higher your score is, the better, but here's the truth: You don't need a perfect 850. Generally, very good credit (or a 740+ FICO Score) is what it takes to earn a lender's best rates (along with a high income, low debt-to-income ratio, and overall financial stability). Depending on where you're starting, 740 may seem impossible, but you can get there if you have a plan, perseverance, and time. This chapter takes you through sound strategies to fix some of the mistakes you may have made in your credit history, while pointing you to more drastic solutions if necessary.

PAYING OFF DEBT

Get That Albatross from Around Your Neck

Using a card to borrow money to pay bills and to build up for miles, rewards, and other benefits is a perfect way to leverage debt. But for many, debt is a source of stress, not financial strength. It can be difficult or nearly impossible to improve credit if you're buried under a mountain of high-interest debt. Thankfully, there are many effective strategies that can release overburdened borrowers from their monetary chains.

This entry examines the debt snowball, the debt avalanche, and the debt snowflake methods. These are not the only tactics to pay off debt, but they are proven effective and easy to understand. Before moving forward, it's essential to note that each strategy requires you to make at least the minimum monthly payment on all of your debt bills. Otherwise, you'll take a hit to your payment history and, in turn, your credit score. Also, regardless of how the math immediately shakes out, the best debt paydown strategy is the one you can stay consistent with over the long term.

THREE POPULAR DEBT PAYDOWN STRATEGIES

There are three popular debt paydown strategies of note in this entry. The first, the debt snowball, involves paying the lowest balance debt first. The second, the debt avalanche, focuses on paying your highest-interest debt first. And the last, the debt snowflake, focuses on cutting your spending and putting the savings toward a debt of your choosing.

The Debt Snowball

Think about what happens when you roll a snowball downhill. As you push, it starts to grow, and as it grows, it gains momentum, eventually rolling without your help. At this point, the snowball has enough heft that it can roll down the hill using its own weight. The debt snowball method is based on this idea.

The snowball requires you to focus on your debt with the lowest balances first, regardless of annual percentage rates (APRs). It might feel strange prioritizing small debts over high rates, but lining up several smaller wins (especially at the start of your debt payoff journey) can be the spark you need to keep the veritable snowball rolling. Completely paying off a debt is a psychological win. Prioritizing smaller debts means easier wins, and the more wins you have, the more dedicated you will become to getting rid of your debt.

To illustrate, let's say that you pay about $500 in total each month in minimum payments across three credit cards as follows:

- Card one: $10,000 balance and 21.99% APR
- Card two: $4,000 balance and 29.99% APR
- Card three: $3,000 balance and 17.99% APR

After you pay your $500 in minimum payments, you have $100 left in your budget to put toward your credit card debt. If you were following the debt snowball method, you would put the entire $100 on card three, because it's the one with the smallest balance. Once you pay off that card, you'd move on to card two, and so forth.

The Debt Avalanche

The debt avalanche requires you to make extra payments on your debt with the highest APRs, no matter the size of the balance. That means in the previous scenario, you would put the extra $100 on card two, since it has the highest APR.

The debt avalanche can take a little more mental toughness than the debt snowball. If your highest-interest debt is also your largest, you may be paying extra on the same debt for a long, long time. For some, this can be demoralizing, as it may be several years before you completely pay off a single debt bill. Still, you will have the knowledge that you are tackling your "scariest" (most expensive) debt first, which can provide a sense of relief.

Snowball versus Avalanche

LendingTree conducted a study to see which method, the snowball or the avalanche, saves more interest and can get you out of debt faster. According to its findings, as long as you have an average amount of debt, both methods yield about the same results.

The Debt Snowflake

The debt snowflake method is a little less rigid than the avalanche and snowball methods. It works best when used in tandem with the snowball or avalanche, but if you can't swing both, snowflaking can be a good place to start. The idea behind this strategy is that you will "snowflake" little extra debt payments here and there by finding extra money in your daily budget.

The best thing about debt snowflaking is that it's easy to implement, even if you don't have a ton of extra money at the end of the month. Instead, you'll try to find little ways you can save every day and then put that savings toward debt. This debt payoff strategy can also help shift your mindset into savings mode and cement smarter spending habits.

Imagine that, just for a month, you promise yourself that you'll make coffee at home instead of buying it on your way to work. After the thirty-day challenge, you do the math and learn that you've been spending $75 a month on coffee without really thinking about it. You can then take that $75 and put it toward whatever debt you choose, whether it's low-balance or high-interest debt. There are tons of little ways that can help you save big, whether it's dealing with a cooler house during winter and putting the utility bill savings toward debt, or riding your bike to work so you can put your gas money toward debt. Examine your lifestyle, figure out what areas you could cut back in, and then snowflake those extra funds to the creditors you owe.

MASTERING CREDIT UTILIZATION RATIO

Finding the Sweet Spot

This book has touched on the concept of credit utilization (how much revolving credit you're currently using compared to how much you have available) several times, but having a deep understanding of this concept alerts you to the major influence it has on your amounts-owed credit scoring factor. Amounts owed makes up 30% of a FICO Score and is the second most important metric, behind payment history. This entry examines the nuances behind credit utilization and how this scoring factor impacts your credit.

UNDERSTANDING CREDIT UTILIZATION RATIO

Credit utilization ratio measures how much revolving debt a borrower has compared to how much they have available. It's represented as a percentage—the higher the percentage, the worse for the borrower. Remember that revolving credit only includes open-ended credit, like credit cards and personal lines of credit. It does not include installment loans like auto loans or mortgages, as those are forms of closed-ended credit. To better understand how credit utilization works, let's say you have one credit card, and it's your only revolving debt. The credit card has a $3,000 balance and a $10,000 limit. In that case, your credit utilization score is 30%.

Generally, a credit utilization ratio above 30% is a red flag that the borrower is stretched thin by the debt they already have.

There are two ways that lenders calculate credit utilization ratio. If the borrower only has one card or form of revolving credit, then the lender will of course only use that card to calculate credit utilization ratio. But if the borrower has more than one, lenders can also consider all of the borrower's cards and calculate credit utilization as a whole. For that reason, it doesn't usually help your credit utilization score if you have a card that's nearly maxed out and another with a low balance.

So, does that mean the perfect credit utilization ratio is 0%? Not exactly. A 0% credit utilization ratio doesn't give lenders or their underwriting algorithm enough information to accurately determine a borrower's risk. When a lender can't assess risk, it will be leery to extend credit, and if it does, rates will be high.

What Is a Good Credit Utilization Ratio?

Unlike credit scores, credit utilization ratios don't have ranges that are ranked with labels like good and bad. Generally, lenders like to see a credit utilization ratio under 36%, but a single-digit ratio is best. According to an Experian study, people with exceptional credit scores have an average credit utilization ratio of about 7%.

- Exceptional (800–850): 7.1%
- Very good (740–799): 15.2%
- Good (670–739): 38.6%
- Fair (580–669): 61.4%
- Poor (300–579): 80.7%

HOW TO IMPROVE CREDIT UTILIZATION RATIO

Now that you know how important credit utilization ratio is, the following are some tips that will help you to improve it.

Pay Off Current Debt

The simplest (but not necessarily easiest) way to improve credit utilization is to pay down current revolving debt. Target the account that has the highest balance and begin to pay more than the minimum amount due, while not neglecting other bills.

Pay Before Your Statement Date

Understanding when credit card issuers report payments to the credit bureaus is essential when improving credit score ratio. There are three main dates to remember when it comes to credit card billing cycles:

- **Statement date:** In order to bill you, credit card issuers add up all of the charges you made during the month. This is called your statement (or closing) date. Any charges that you make after your statement date go on the next month's bill. A statement balance is how much you owe after any payments you may have made while in the middle of your billing cycle.
- **Due date:** You have to pay at least the minimum amount due on your due date. Otherwise, the credit card company will consider your payment late.
- **Reporting date:** Your credit card issuer reports your payments to the credit bureaus on your reporting date. The issuer does

not specify its reporting date on your bill, but most report right around your statement date.

Consider making credit card payments intermittently throughout the month and before your statement date. If you do, the credit card company will have a lower total balance to report, and as a result your credit utilization ratio will be lower. As a bonus, what you pay off won't be subject to interest. Interest only applies on credit cards when you carry a balance from billing cycle to billing cycle.

Ask for a Credit Line Increase

Another way to lower your credit utilization ratio is by increasing your available credit. You may request a credit line increase on an existing credit card, for example. Keep in mind that your credit card company will likely only agree if you have a positive payment history and if your credit report doesn't show that you are already overburdened by debt. Also, find out whether your credit card company uses a hard or soft credit inquiry after you request a line increase, as this varies by issuer. After six to twelve months of responsible use, your credit card company might automatically increase your spending power. If it does, it will only use a soft credit hit since you must give your permission before any entity can conduct a hard credit inquiry.

Open a New Credit Card

Another way to decrease your credit utilization ratio is to open a new credit card. This will result in a hard credit inquiry, which can drop your credit score a little. However, consistent on-time payments and the positive impact to your credit utilization ratio is likely to make up for the hard credit inquiry. **Beware: Opening a new credit card or requesting a credit line increase to improve your credit utilization ratio takes discipline.** Having more credit available could lead to overborrowing.

Become an Authorized User on a Credit Card

Getting added as an authorized user can improve your credit utilization ratio, but only if the primary cardholder is using an appropriate amount of their available credit on the card you're being added to.

TIPS TO HELP YOU MAINTAIN A GOOD CREDIT UTILIZATION RATIO

Though a good credit utilization ratio may be hard to maintain, there are a few essential tips to do this easily. For example, you may find that getting a text alert every time your credit card hits a certain balance (even if it's well below your spending limit) can help nudge you to pay off some or all of your credit card bill before your statement date. That means you will have more available credit and a lower balance by the time your credit card issuer reports to the credit bureaus. Additionally, unless you're having a hard time sticking to your budget, it's not a good idea to close out old credit card accounts, even if you rarely use them. Closing an old account means less available credit, and less available credit means existing balances will have a larger impact on your credit utilization ratio. If you have an older, rarely used card, be sure to use it every so often, as most issuers will close accounts after a prolonged period of inactivity.

DISPUTING ERRORS ON YOUR CREDIT REPORT

Don't Get Dinged for Outdated or Incorrect Info

Imagine you're at a car dealership getting ready to buy a new vehicle when the loan officer comes back with some bad news: Your credit report shows two recent late payments, and because of that, the interest rate on your car loan has shot up by 5%. You're shocked. You've never made a late payment in your life. You decide to wait on the car and instead you go home and order your credit report. Lo and behold, the dealer was right. You see two late payments on an account you don't recognize. Upon closer examination, you see that these aren't your payments. They're your dad's. You're a junior and he's a senior.

This is called a mixed or merged credit file, and it happens when a credit bureau mistakenly combines your credit history with someone else's. This can happen if two borrowers share a name, have similar Social Security numbers, or share contact information like address and phone number. Throughout this entry, you'll find the most common errors and how to deal with them.

How to Order Your Credit Reports

Order one free credit report a week from each of the three bureaus at www.annualcreditreport.com. Order them before applying for a loan to check for errors, and periodically look for suspicious changes.

COMMON CREDIT
REPORTING ERRORS

The first step in disputing a credit reporting error is recognizing the error in the first place. Each credit report has a slightly different way of presenting information. Reports can also be organized differently depending on where you ordered them (directly through the bureau itself or through a third-party service). Here are some common errors to look out for, and where you can find them on your credit report.

Identity Errors

An identity error is a mistake in your name, date of birth, Social Security number, phone number, address, or occupation. A small typo in your name can cause big problems, like in our previous example of mixed or merged files. You can review your identity information in the PII (personally identifiable information) section of your credit report. This will be the first section of your credit report.

Account Errors

Any incorrect information regarding tradelines, payment history, account balances, and borrowing history could be an account error. Look for missing payments, late payments, and incorrect balances. You may see these filed under "adverse accounts"; look for payment history under "satisfactory accounts."

Fraud or Identity Theft

Take some extra time and look for any accounts that you don't recognize. Unexplained accounts or credit inquiries could be due to a fraudster using your sensitive information to take out loans and cards.

Public Records Errors

In 2017, the three credit bureaus removed most civil judgements from their reports. A civil judgement is the end result of a civil lawsuit. If you find any civil judgements on your report, scrutinize them carefully and consider disputing them. The three credit bureaus also agreed to remove all tax liens from their reports in 2018. You shouldn't see any tax liens on your report (even if they belong to you), so dispute any you might find.

Inquiry Errors

Look over the recent inquiry section of your credit report and look for unexplained hard credit hits. Note that if you use a free credit score service like Credit Karma, you will likely see lots of soft credit inquiries. These services run a soft inquiry on a regular cadence in order to provide you with up-to-date scores. But if you see hard credit inquires that you don't recognize or that should not be counted as one due to the rate shopping window, dispute them.

HOW TO DISPUTE A CREDIT REPORT ERROR

Disputing a credit report error is fairly straightforward. Equifax, Experian, and TransUnion all allow consumers to dispute errors on their websites. To register a dispute:

- For Equifax, visit www.equifax.com/personal/credit-report-services/credit-dispute or call (866) 349-5191.

- For Experian, visit www.experian.com/help/dispute-credit or call (888) 397-3742.
- For TransUnion, visit www.transunion.com/credit-disputes/dispute-your-credit or call (800) 916-8800.

It's also possible to dispute credit report errors via snail mail, but expect the process to take longer since the bureau won't start investigating until it has received your request. Depending on what you're disputing, you may need to provide the credit bureau with supporting documentation. You'll need proof of identity, like a government-issued ID, if you're trying to get your name corrected. Or the bureau might need to see a police report in cases of identity theft. In any case, take care to follow the instructions the bureau gives you to avoid any hiccups in the process.

WHAT HAPPENS AFTER THE DISPUTE?

A certain set of actions are triggered as soon as the credit bureau receives your dispute. Here's what happens behind the scenes.

The Bureau Receives Your Dispute

Under the Fair Credit Reporting Act, a credit bureau has thirty days to complete its investigation, although it may have up to forty-five if you also sent in supporting documents. The bureau can ignore certain disputes, including those that don't have enough information for the bureau to start the process, so be very clear in what you're disputing and provide as much documentation as you can. The bureau can also decline to investigate disputes that it perceives as fraudulent. If it declines to investigate, it must send you a letter within five business days explaining why.

The Dispute Goes to the "Furnisher"

A furnisher is whatever company, lender, or other entity that you claim is listing incorrect information. For example, if the borrower disputes an incorrectly listed late payment, the credit bureau will send the dispute to the lender that reported said late payment.

The Bureau Makes Its Decision

If the furnisher can't verify whether the disputed information is true, then it must tell the credit bureau, and the bureau must remove it from the borrower's credit report. Or the furnisher may prove to the bureau that the disputed information is indeed correct. Depending on the outcome, the disputed information may remain on the borrower's credit report or be removed. Either way, the bureau is required to send a letter to the borrower letting them know whether or not their dispute was successful, and if it wasn't, why.

RAPID RESCORING

Get a Better Mortgage Rate, Fast

Buying a home requires strong credit. According to Experian, the average credit score for someone with a mortgage is 758. These kinds of numbers can take a long time to build. Often, potential homebuyers spend months, if not years, chipping away at current debt and avoiding hard inquiries to boost their credit ahead of a mortgage application. This is where rapid rescoring can help. This lesser-known strategy can offer a quick credit score boost during the home-buying process.

WHAT IS RAPID RESCORING?

Pretend that you're in the process of buying a house. Your mortgage broker lets you know that it will take about thirty days from application to close. While they're looking over your credit reports, they notice that you have a sizeable balance on one of your credit cards, and it's dragging down your score. Your score is 720, which is good (on the cusp of very good). Your broker tells you that you're close to qualifying for a lower mortgage rate, but that you would need to significantly pay down (or pay off) that credit card. If you can make a big payment, the broker says they'll have your lender do a rapid rescore afterward. But what is rapid rescoring?

Rapid rescoring is a way to get the credit bureaus to update the information on your credit report quicker than usual. Under normal circumstances, updates happen once a month. That means it takes at least a month for actions like paying off debt to make a difference in your credit. Rapid rescoring shortens this window to as few as three to five business days. Like in this example, homebuyers typically benefit from rapid rescoring if they pay down debt during the mortgage process, or if they successfully dispute a credit reporting error. Depending on the action the borrower takes, rapid rescoring can boost a homebuyer's credit score by as much as one hundred points.

Ask for Rapid Rescoring by Name

If you're interested in rapid rescoring, tell your mortgage broker. Consumers can't request a rapid rescore, only lenders can. If you aren't using a broker, ask your prospective mortgage lender instead.

COSTS ASSOCIATED WITH RAPID RESCORING

Rapid rescoring isn't free. Each rescore costs $25–$40 per credit bureau and per credit line. For instance, if a borrower wants a rapid rescore because they paid off two credit cards, the total cost of the rapid rescore would be $150 (assuming the low-end cost of $25). Two credit lines = $50 per credit report × 3 (for the three main credit bureaus: Equifax, Experian, and TransUnion).

While rapid rescoring isn't free, it shouldn't cost the homebuyer. The Fair Credit Reporting Act prohibits lenders and credit bureaus from charging consumers when they dispute errors on their credit report. Rapid rescoring falls under this umbrella. Lenders are also not allowed to fold rapid rescoring expenses into closing costs. Not all lenders offer rapid rescoring, because they don't want to eat these expenses. However, if your mortgage broker truly believes that you would benefit from rapid rescoring, they may steer you toward a lender that is rapid rescoring–friendly. After all, the broker gets a commission for each loan they close, and you'll get a lower rate as a bonus.

WHAT'S NEEDED FOR RAPID RESCORING?

The homebuyer must provide certain documentation in order for a credit bureau to run a rapid rescore. These documents prove that the homebuyer resolved a credit issue that could be holding them back from a better rate, and the docs serve as evidence that a rapid rescore really could result in an upward swing in the buyer's credit score. Brokers and lenders will know more about what paperwork is needed, as it's very situational. Generally, though, homebuyers can expect to provide:

- Letters from credit card issuers and other lenders showing that a debt has been paid (must be on company letterhead)
- Screenshots from online statements showing recent debt payments
- Bankruptcy discharge paperwork
- Letters from collection accounts, on company letterhead
- Credit release forms from card issuers (specifically, American Express)

That said, some lenders offer "no-doc" services. For an additional cost, the bureau will use an automated system to confirm current credit card balances and recent payments. No-doc services typically only apply if the homebuyer has made a large debt payment that they'd like considered, not if they are attempting to remove incorrect information or late payments from their credit report.

What about Rapid Rescoring for Other Loans?

Unfortunately, rapid rescoring only applies to mortgage loans. If you're planning on applying for an auto loan, personal loan, or credit card, you should take other steps to improve your score first, like reviewing and disputing credit reporting errors.

THE ALL ZERO EXCEPT ONE ALTERNATIVE

Borrowers looking for a quick credit score boost before applying for a mortgage sometimes employ AZEO, or the all zero except one strategy. To use AZEO, the borrower must have balances across multiple credit cards, the means to pay off almost all of their credit card debt in one fell swoop, and about a month to wait for their credit reports to update.

When following AZEO, a borrower pays off all of their credit cards except for one. On that one card, they will then carry a small balance, typically less than $100—but only long enough for that balance to be reported to the credit bureaus. After it's been reported, the borrower will pay off the balance to avoid unnecessary interest.

Depending on how much revolving debt the borrower currently has (and what they have available to them), AZEO can help a borrower hit that coveted single-digit credit utilization percentage (how much of their available revolving credit they're using) without dropping their ratio to O. It seems counterintuitive, but lenders don't like to see a O credit utilization ratio. They need data and a proven track record of responsible credit use in order to predict a borrower's future risk.

DEBT CONSOLIDATION

Savings Tool or Shell Game?

Debt consolidation is a personal finance strategy that can help borrowers who are juggling multiple credit cards and personal loan bills. Debt consolidation is the act of taking out one new loan or credit card and using it to pay off several smaller debts. The process doesn't change the amount of principal the borrower owes. Instead, it reorganizes it. Consolidating can be beneficial when executed correctly, but it can also lead borrowers to dig themselves further into the hole if they aren't careful.

HOW DEBT CONSOLIDATION WORKS

Also called debt refinancing or credit card refinancing, debt consolidation requires the borrower to take out one new, larger debt and use it to pay off several smaller debts. Once the smaller debts have been paid, the borrower will only have one debt bill on their plate: their debt consolidation bill. Most people consolidate by using a debt consolidation loan (a type of personal loan, typically unsecured), but balance transfer credit cards and home equity loans are also popular choices. Only unsecured debt can be consolidated, including credit cards, personal loans, medical bills, and student loans.

Be Careful Consolidating Student Loans

If you're thinking about consolidating federal student loans with a private student loan, reconsider. Some borrower protections like income-driven repayment plans are specific to federal student loans. You'll lose these by consolidating with a private loan.

HOW DEBT CONSOLIDATION CAN IMPROVE CREDIT

There are several ways that debt consolidation can improve your credit. A few of the following are outlined here.

It Can Reduce Credit Utilization Ratio

Credit utilization ratio measures how much revolving debt a borrower has compared to how much credit they have available. Credit cards are revolving debt, and debt consolidation loans and home equity loans are installment debt. Replace a significant amount of revolving debt with installment debt, and you could see a dramatic improvement in credit utilization ratio. Credit utilization ratio is part of FICO's amounts-owed credit scoring factor, and amounts owed makes up 30% of a FICO Score.

It Can Streamline Your Budget

Instead of keeping track of multiple monthly debt payments, borrowers only have one bill to pay after consolidating: their debt consolidation loan, balance transfer credit card, or home equity loan bill. This can make it less likely that a bill falls through the cracks, simply because the borrower will have less of them. Payment history makes up 35% of a FICO Score.

It Can Diversify Credit Mix

As long as the borrower doesn't close all of their credit cards after consolidating, debt consolidation could diversify credit mix if a debt consolidation loan is the borrower's first or only installment loan. Credit mix makes up 10% of a FICO Score.

It Can Become Easier to Build an Emergency Fund

Consolidating debt can indirectly help a borrower improve their credit score by giving them the resources needed to build an emergency fund. Consolidating might bring down a borrower's monthly debt bill if they qualify for a lower interest rate or if they choose a longer repayment term. These extra monthly savings could do well in an emergency fund—an essential piece of the puzzle that is good credit.

HOW DEBT CONSOLIDATION CAN HURT CREDIT

Though it can be helpful, debt consolidation can also hurt your credit. A few of the ways it can are outlined here.

It Brings Down Average Age of Accounts

Any new loan or card will lower the average age of a borrower's credit accounts. But debt consolidation becomes a larger issue if the borrower also closes their credit cards after paying them off with the new loan or card. Ideally, the borrower should keep their cards open and use them infrequently for small purchases to help keep up the average age of their accounts. However, if the cards pose too much of a temptation, it's best to cancel them and take the hit. Length of credit history is only 15% of a FICO Score, while payment history is 35%.

It Requires a Hard Credit Inquiry

Borrowers need to agree to a hard credit inquiry when applying for most loans. A hard credit inquiry can negatively impact a credit score, but only a little. For most, one hard credit inquiry will drop a credit score by five points or less. Hard credit inquiries show on a credit report for two years, but scores usually rebound within a year. The number of hard inquiries a borrower has affects new credit, which contributes 10% to a FICO Score.

It Doesn't Change Poor Spending Habits

Debt consolidation doesn't address the elephant in the room: poor spending habits. If someone pays off their credit cards with a loan but doesn't stop using the cards, they're only digging themselves further into debt. Consolidating debt without examining the reason behind the debt is a dangerous combination.

HOW MUCH MONEY CAN DEBT CONSOLIDATION SAVE?

If you're trading in higher-interest debt for lower-interest debt, you could save a significant amount of money. Imagine that you have three credit cards:

- Card A has a 29% APR.
- Card B has a 31% APR.
- Card C has a 33% APR.

This means that you're paying an average APR of 31% across all cards. If you get a debt consolidation loan with an APR below 31%, you'll save on total interest, assuming you don't pick a longer loan term. Look for a debt consolidation calculator online (there are plenty), crunch numbers, and see how consolidating can affect your bottom line.

DEALING WITH DEBT COLLECTORS

You Have More Power Than You Think

When a borrower is late by 90–120 days (the timeline varies), lenders, utilities companies, and other furnishers usually give up collecting what is owed. Instead, they'll sell the debt to a debt collection agency for much less than what the debt is worth. This way, the lender can recover a little bit of the money that they lost. Once the debt is sold, the borrower can expect the debt collection agency to attempt to collect via phone calls, letters, and lawsuits.

The debt collector must always remain professional, thanks to the Fair Debt Collection Practices Act.

THE FAIR DEBT COLLECTION PRACTICES ACT (FDCPA)

Passed in 1977 by former President Jimmy Carter, the FDCPA protects consumers from abusive debt collection practices. To be compliant with the FDCPA, debt collectors can't:

- Contact you before 8 a.m. or after 9 p.m. unless you say it's okay.
- Contact you at work if you tell them to stop.
- Email you, text you, or message you on social media if you tell them to stop.
- Create public social media posts or publish lists of those who owe debt.

- Call more than seven times in seven days or call within seven days after talking to you about a specific debt (also known as the 7-in-7 rule).
- Threaten legal action if they know legal action cannot be taken.
- Fail to disclose that they are a debt collector (in most cases).
- Claim to be an attorney, work for the government, or work in law enforcement if untrue.
- Collect anything other than what you truly owe based on your contract (principal, interest, and fees).
- Send letters in envelopes that indicate that the letter is in reference to a collection attempt.
- Coerce you to write a post-dated check or accept a check that is post-dated more than five days in the future without written notification.

The FDCPA Doesn't Apply to All Debt Calls

The FDCPA only applies to debt collection agencies, not the original creditor. For example, if Discover calls you over a past due credit card balance, the FDCPA doesn't apply. But you are protected by the FDCPA if Discover sells that debt to a third-party collection agency.

YOUR RIGHT TO VALIDATE DEBT

The FDCPA also gives consumers the right to validate the debt the agency is attempting to collect. This is very important. Within five days of contacting you, the debt collection agency must send you a debt validation letter. A debt validation letter will tell you what debt collection agency is working on your file, information about the original creditor you may owe, what you can do if you think the debt isn't yours, and your rights under the FDCPA. You have thirty days to dispute the debt if it isn't yours or you suspect the debt is no longer collectible due to the statute of limitations. If you don't dispute the debt within this timeframe, that debt is now yours.

Never Admit a Debt Is Yours Without Validating It First

It's illegal, but some debt collectors may threaten or attempt to sue over debt that is beyond its statute of limitations. The debt may still show on your credit report and you still technically owe it, but debt collectors can't sue you for debt that is legally past a certain age.

Before acknowledging that a debt belongs to you, check your state's laws regarding time-barred debt. Time-barred debt is debt that has surpassed its statute of limitations. The statute of limitations on debt depends on state law as well as the type of debt. Some debts (like federal student loans) don't have a statute of limitations. And tax debts have a longer statute of limitations than consumer debts, like credit card debt. The "clock" on time-barred debt typically begins from the date of your first missed payment. Even if the debt collector can't sue you over time-barred debt, acknowledging that the debt is yours or making a payment on old debt can restart the time-barred debt clock and make the debt suable again.

HANDLING DEBT COLLECTOR CALLS

The first thing to do if you get a call from a debt collector is to ask for a validation letter, but do not admit that the debt is yours and do not give out any personal information. Next, try the following.

Keep Meticulous Records

Any time a debt collector calls, write down the name of the debt collection agency, the name of the agent, the time the call took place, and the details of the call. If you end up going to court, this log could come in handy.

Respond to Any Court Summons

Even if the debt is not yours or you've already paid it, ignoring a court summons can be disastrous. If you fail to appear in court, the judge is likely to side with the debt collection agency without giving you the opportunity to plead your case. If this happens, you may have a money judgement issued against you. A money judgement allows debt collection agencies to take more aggressive measures in collecting the debt including wage garnishment, bank levies, or property liens. A bank levy is similar to a wage garnishment, but instead of taking the funds out of your paycheck, the debt collector can freeze your bank account and seize funds from it.

If the Debt Is Yours, Consider Negotiating

Once you've confirmed that the debt is yours, you could try to settle for less than you owe. You can do this yourself for free, or you can pay a debt settlement company to attempt to negotiate on your behalf. Consider trying the DIY route first to avoid settlement fees.

Contact an Attorney

You may want to contact a lawyer if you believe your rights have been violated or if the agency is attempting to sue over time-barred debt. If you obtain legal representation, the debt collection agency is required to work with them instead of you. If anything, this can help take some stress off your shoulders.

NONPROFIT CREDIT COUNSELING

Work with a Pro to Get Out of Debt

Overwhelmed borrowers often turn to debt settlement, credit repair, or bankruptcy to get out of debt. Not only will these options nuke their credit score, but some options—namely debt settlement and credit repair—can leave the borrower worse off than when they started. Credit counseling is a safe, low-cost alternative.

WHAT IS CREDIT COUNSELING?

You can think of credit counseling as financial therapy. Borrowers work with trained, certified professionals to improve their financial situation through education and guidance. Sessions usually last about an hour and can take place in person, over the phone, or online. How many sessions the borrower attends depends on their needs and goals, which they will determine with the credit counselor's help. Many credit counseling agencies offer free educational resources and only charge fees for specific services, such as debt management plans.

It can be easy to confuse credit counseling with other for-profit services like debt settlement, partially because many debt settlement companies present themselves as credit counseling services. Some less-reputable credit counseling agencies may also offer debt settlement as a service. If you're considering credit counseling, make sure that the agency you choose is legit. Some trusted agencies include:

- **The National Foundation for Credit Counseling (NFCC):** Founded in 1951, the NFCC is America's oldest and largest credit counseling agency. You can visit its website at www.nfcc.org.
- **The Financial Counseling Association of America (FCAA):** The FCAA is another trusted nonprofit organization, founded in 1993. Learn more at www.fcaa.org.
- **The U.S. Department of Justice (DOJ):** The DOJ also maintains a database of approved credit counseling agencies at www.justice.gov/ust/list-credit-counseling-agencies-approved-pursuant-11-usc-111.

Though, as stated previously, there are other credit counseling agencies out there, the sources listed are vetted and legitimate.

SERVICES AVAILABLE THROUGH CREDIT COUNSELING

Credit counseling is helpful in a variety of different scenarios and can provide services tailored to your situation.

Assistance with Budgeting

Credit counseling agencies offer general financial literacy classes and personalized budgeting. Importantly, a credit counselor can help a borrower get to the root cause of their debt, helping the borrower create positive, long-lasting changes in their financial situation.

Debt Management Plans

One of the most common reasons why borrowers sign up for credit counseling is to enroll in a debt management plan (DMP). A DMP is a prerequisite to filing for bankruptcy, but declaring bankruptcy isn't required to enroll in a DMP. There are no minimum debt requirements when it comes to DMPs. To qualify, the borrower must earn enough income to cover their debt, but not so much that the credit counselor determines that the borrower can pay off their debt without the help of a DMP.

A DMP is a three-to-five-year repayment plan that can help a borrower pay off unsecured debt stemming from credit cards, personal loans, and medical bills. The counselor will work with the borrower's creditors, usually to reduce late fees, interest rates, and/or the borrower's monthly payments through loan modification (extending a loan term, for example). However, a DMP doesn't reduce the principal the borrower owes. It restructures it (similar to debt consolidation).

How Much Does Credit Counseling Cost?

Some aspects of credit counseling might be free, such as generalized financial literacy classes. But DMPs come at a modest cost. A one-time setup fee between $25 and $75 is typical, and monthly fees cannot exceed $79 according to federal law. States may also have their own individual caps and regulations.

Instead of paying off each debt on their own, the borrower will give their debt payment to the credit counselor. The credit counselor then pays the borrower's creditors on their behalf, taking some of the burden off of the borrower. Enrolling in a DMP can also stop debt lawsuits and incessant phone calls from creditors.

When a borrower is under a DMP, they can no longer use the credit cards that are enrolled in the plan. Applying for new credit is also strongly discouraged.

CREDIT COUNSELING'S IMPACT ON CREDIT SCORES

Signing up for credit counseling doesn't impact the borrower's credit score. At least not directly. However, actions taken during credit counseling can, mostly in a positive way. A professionally created budget will ideally help the borrower get back on track with debt payments, and on-time payments are integral to improving credit. At 35%, payment history is the most important factor of a FICO Score. Credit utilization ratio—or how much revolving debt a borrower owes compared to how much credit they have available—will presumably go down as the borrower pays off their debts. When it comes to credit utilization, lower is generally better.

Still, enrolling in a DMP can temporarily hurt a borrower's credit score because it involves closing the credit accounts the borrower enrolls in the plan. Age of accounts is a FICO Score factor, but it's much less important than payment history (15% compared to 35%). The credit counselor may also make a note on the borrower's credit report, indicating that the borrower is enrolled in a DMP. Future lenders will be able to see this note, but how this note affects their underwriting decisions is up to the lender.

That said, borrowers should take the long view. Generally, the actions a borrower takes during credit counseling will improve the borrower's credit over time. Any company—whether it be a credit counseling agency or debt settlement company—that promises quick, positive results is likely a scam.

The positive impact of credit counseling also depends on the borrower's dedication to the program. Borrowers can drop out of credit counseling at any time, and many do. Nonprofit agency DebtWave Credit Counseling conducted a five-year study on DMPs and found that 68.4% of the enrollees it tracked successfully completed their DMPs. Of those who dropped out, most simply stopped making payments. The second-largest group to drop out ended up filing for bankruptcy.

WHEN BANKRUPTCY MAY BE THE RIGHT CHOICE

A Fresh Start for Those Who Need It

Borrowers who are truly buried in debt with no realistic path forward may need to consider bankruptcy. Bankruptcy can be a hard pill to swallow, but borrowers shouldn't let unfair stigma stop them from taking the steps necessary to regain control of their finances. Bankruptcy exists for a reason, and hundreds of thousands of people file each year—including nearly half a million in 2024 alone (494,201, according to the U.S. Federal Courts). Still, bankruptcy has a dramatic impact on credit for up to a decade. It's not a decision to take lightly, or one to make without the help of a professional. The information here is a high-level overview of this very complicated topic.

WHAT IS BANKRUPTCY?

Bankruptcy is a legal process that can forgive some or all of a borrower's debt. There are six types of bankruptcy, each named after its corresponding chapter in the U.S. bankruptcy code. For individuals, Chapter 7 and Chapter 13 bankruptcy are the most common. Other chapters mostly pertain to businesses or entire municipalities, like cities and towns.

If you've never been there, it's easy to assume that bankruptcy is the result of irresponsibility. In reality, uncontrollable life events like medical problems, job loss, and divorce are often the trigger.

Regardless of the reason, filing for bankruptcy will provide an immediate reprieve from debt collection calls, lawsuits, and wage garnishments. This is called an automatic stay. An automatic stay can also stop a mortgage lender from foreclosing on a home or an auto lender from repossessing a car, but only if the borrower continues making payments while their bankruptcy case is active. What happens after the automatic stay depends on the type of bankruptcy that was filed.

Bankruptcy Requires Mandatory Credit Counseling

Borrowers must complete credit counseling through an approved agency within 180 days before filing for either Chapter 7 or Chapter 13. Learn more about credit counseling in the previous entry, "Nonprofit Credit Counseling."

CHAPTER 7 BANKRUPTCY

Also known as liquidation bankruptcy, Chapter 7 requires the borrower to sell assets and use the proceeds to pay off debt, which is handled through a court-appointed trustee. Then, any eligible debt left over is forgiven. This might not sound like a fair shake. How can the courts expect someone to survive without a car or house? The good news is that they don't. Some types of personal property are exempt from Chapter 7 liquidation. In fact, most Chapter 7 cases are "no asset," which means the filer didn't own any nonexempt assets. If someone owns a lot of nonexempt assets (like second homes, cash, and/or investments), then they would likely file for Chapter 13 instead.

Chapter 7 Asset Exemptions

Exemptions are determined at both the state and federal level. In most states, the state itself decides whether you can use state or federal exemptions. A handful of states let you choose between state and federal but importantly, only state or only federal exemptions will apply. In other words, you can't claim some property under state exemption and other under federal.

Federal bankruptcy exemptions protect the following types of property:

- Car ($5,025)
- Home equity, but only if the home is your principal residence ($31,575)
- Jewelry ($2,125)
- Personal property, like household items, clothes, animals, crops, and musical instruments ($800 per individual item, with an overall limit of $16,850)
- Tools of the trade ($3,175)
- Life insurance policies and accrued dividends ($16,850)
- Prescribed medical devices (fully exempt)
- Public benefits, like Social Security and unemployment (fully exempt)
- Child support and alimony (fully exempt)
- Retirement accounts (401(k)s, 403(b)s, and pensions are fully exempt; IRAs and Roth IRAs are exempt up to $1,711,975 in total, per person)
- Wildcard exemption ($1,675 plus $15,800 of any unused portion of your homestead exemption can be put toward any property of your choosing)

So even though Chapter 7 filers do stand to lose some property, they still won't be left totally penniless. That said, Chapter 7 shows on credit reports for ten years. In that timeframe, it will be especially hard for the filer to qualify for new loans and cards, although it is possible, especially as time passes.

Chapter 7 Eligibility Requirements

Not everyone who wants to file for Chapter 7 can. Before someone can file for Chapter 7, they must pass what's called a means test. If the filer earns more than the median income in their state, they must file paperwork that proves to the court that they truly cannot afford to pay their debt. If they don't pass the means test, they will have to pursue Chapter 13 instead.

Chapter 7 and Secured Loans

Property with a loan is treated differently than items the filer owns outright. To keep these types of properties (like a car with a loan or a house with a mortgage), the filer must "reaffirm the debt" with the lender by agreeing to continue making payments as outlined in the original loan agreement. If the lender agrees, the filer could instead choose to "redeem the property." This requires a lump sum payment for the fair market value of the property rather than the full amount the filer owes. If the Chapter 7 filer is unable to reaffirm the debt or redeem the property, then the lender will repossess the car or foreclose on the house.

CHAPTER 13 BANKRUPTCY

Under Chapter 13 (also called the wage-earner's plan), the filer will pay at least some of their debt through a three-to-five-year repayment plan. In exchange, the filer doesn't have to sell assets. Chapter 13 appears on credit reports for seven years, three years less than Chapter 7. Although Chapter 13 will still likely cause the filer's credit score to plummet, lenders tend to look more favorably on Chapter 13, since the borrower is paying off at least some of their debt.

Chapter 13 Eligibility Requirements

Chapter 13 has its own set of eligibility requirements. Namely, the court must determine that the filer has enough income to pay some of their debt with a repayment plan. The debt must also be under a certain amount, and the filer must put all of their disposable income toward the debt for three to five years. In this context, disposable income is whatever the filer has left over after living expenses.

DISCHARGEABLE DEBTS

Bankruptcy can seem like a magic bullet, albeit a serious one, but it doesn't help with all debt. Not all debt is dischargeable (or eligible to be forgiven) in bankruptcy. Whether a debt is dischargeable or not is determined by bankruptcy law. Specifically, the Bankruptcy Reform Act of 1978, which was amended several times in later years to prevent fraud and abuse. Bankruptcy was designed to give overburdened borrowers a fresh start, and as a result, most consumer debt is dischargeable. However, some debt would be unfair to discharge and could cause hardship for others, such as back child support and/

or alimony. Chapter 13 is a bit broader when it comes to specific debt tied to government fines, property settlements in divorce, and other niche cases. But for the most part, Chapter 7 and Chapter 13 share the same dischargeable and nondischargeable debts.

Dischargeable Debts:

- Unsecured debt (personal loans, medical bills, credit card bills)
- Taxes more than three years old (as long as you filed on time)
- Loans from friends and family
- Past due utilities and rent
- Lawyer fees

Nondischargeable Debts:

- Taxes fewer than three years old
- Child support and alimony
- Federal student loans (usually)
- Criminal fines
- Restitution and personal injury caused by driving under the influence
- Debt caused by willful and malicious injury

Bankruptcy is complicated. Filing comes with years-long implications, not just those that affect the filer's credit report, but also what debt the filer may still owe after declaring bankruptcy, as well as the assets the filer may lose. It's crucial to speak to a bankruptcy attorney when considering this path.

Chapter 6

Maintaining Excellent Credit for Life

Building good credit isn't a one-and-done achievement. It takes a lifetime of work. Credit scores are dynamic and change based on your spending habits, financial decisions, and life events, and, at times, seemingly for no reason. Don't let this get you down. Building and maintaining credit requires years of effort, but it doesn't necessarily have to be hard to do. Small habits can have a big impact, and once you establish those good habits, they may become second nature.

In this chapter, you'll learn strategies that can help you move the needle of your credit score from good to excellent. You'll also review how some common life events can impact your credit score, and you'll learn how you should react to these events to keep your three numbers where you want them to be.

HABITS OF THE 800+ CLUB

The Secret Sauce Behind a Perfect Score

Truth be told, very few things in life require an 800+ credit score. Assuming they tick other boxes, like sufficient income and a longer credit history, borrowers with good credit (670+) qualify for most loans and cards. Those with very good credit (740+) often qualify for the lowest rates (as long as they meet other benchmarks, like earning a high income).

However, even if perfect credit isn't really necessary, that doesn't mean that you shouldn't try. If you already have strong credit, it can be a fun challenge to see how close to 850 you can get. And if your score needs some work, learning the proverbial secret handshake of the 800+ club can get your score moving in the right direction and cement habits that will help you maintain your score for life.

AN 800+ SCORE REQUIRES STAYING ON TOP OF BILLS

Payment history is the single most influential factor in both your FICO Score and your VantageScore. It makes up 35% of the former and 40% of the latter. It's essential to keep up with your payments to earn top-tier credit.

Make More Than One Payment a Month

Borrowers with 800+ credit make credit card payments more than once a month. If they charge something big, they pay off the balance before the charge is reported to maintain a low credit utilization ratio. To do this, these borrowers not only keep track of their due dates but their statement dates too.

Set Text Reminders and Automatic Payments

Agreeing to automatic payments can feel like relinquishing control. However, automatic payments are an excellent safeguard against paying late. But this strategy only works if the money is available in your account when your lender attempts to withdraw what you owe. If the lender offers them, sign up for text reminders to get a heads up when an automatic payment is coming. Instead of text reminders, cell phone calendar reminders also work.

Use Your Credit Card Sparingly

Although you want to keep your credit utilization in the single digits, having a 0 credit utilization ratio isn't ideal. Borrowers with 800+ credit prove to lenders that they can responsibly manage their credit by actually using it.

AN 800+ SCORE REQUIRES USING CREDIT STRATEGICALLY

Perfect-score borrowers don't apply for a store card on a whim for a discount. To have exceptional credit, you need to have a reason behind every card, loan, and swipe.

Treat Credit Cards Like Debit Cards

Only use a credit card if you already have the money to cover the purchase. Credit cards should be a way to earn cashback and rewards, not for floating expenses.

Diversify Your Accounts

An 800+ credit score requires juggling multiple types of credit. Credit mix makes up 10% of a FICO Score. That's why you might see your credit score drop after paying off your car loan.

Keep Old Accounts and Request Credit Increases

The length of your credit history makes up 15% of your FICO Score. For that reason, you shouldn't close a credit card when you pay it off (unless you're having a hard time resisting temptation). Use the card every so often so the issuer doesn't deactivate it, and if your credit utilization begins to creep up, request a credit line increase to even the balance.

Think Like an Underwriter

Obtaining the elusive 800+ credit score can be easier if you think like a loan underwriter. Avoid red-flag behavior like applying for multiple cards in quick succession. This could be a sign that you're struggling financially.

AN 800+ SCORE REQUIRES LONG-TERM PLANNING

Credit scores fluctuate, and life does too. Knowing how to go with the flow—whether up or down—will help you maintain excellent credit for life.

Build an Emergency Fund

No matter your score, keep three to six months' worth of living expenses (or more, depending on your needs) to the side. Layoffs and illnesses rarely come with advance warning.

Don't Be Afraid to Refinance

Refinancing a loan can help you improve or maintain your credit score. Choose a shorter term to pay off a loan faster, as long as you can afford a higher monthly payment. If your financial situation has changed for the worse, refinancing to a longer term will give you a lower monthly payment. This will, however, lead to more total interest.

Talk to an Advisor at Major Financial Crossroads

It may be a good idea to meet with a fiduciary when facing a life change. For instance, your financial goals will likely shift if you're expanding your family or when you're getting close to retirement. Advisor fees may be worth it if you're able to grow wealth, just beware of snake oil salesmen. Look for certified financial planners (CFPs), chartered financial analysts (CFAs), and certified public accountants (CPAs).

AN 800+ SCORE REQUIRES PROTECTING WHAT YOU'VE BUILT

Credit isn't set-it-and-forget-it. Building and keeping exceptional credit takes vigilance, proactivity, and cautious decisions.

Freeze Your Credit

Put a padlock on your credit by freezing it with all three bureaus. No one—including you—can apply for a new loan or card under your name when your credit is frozen. Freezing and unfreezing only takes a few minutes and will keep intruders from tarnishing your good credit.

Check Your Credit Reports

Keep your finger on the pulse by checking your credit reports on a regular basis. You can order one free Equifax, Experian, and TransUnion report each week. Dispute errors and look for suspicious activity that could be a sign of identity theft.

Strongly Reconsider Cosigning

Cosigning is a valid way to help someone build credit, but just because someone asks doesn't mean you have to say yes. Late payments will affect your credit just as much as theirs. You may only want to cosign if you're the one making payments (like if you're helping your child build credit). You could co-borrow instead. Although you'll still be on the hook for payments, you'll have equal ownership of whatever the loan bought.

MAINTAIN A BUDGET

Making Every Dollar Count

The first step toward excellent credit is to build a budget. A proper budget should stop you from having to take on expensive or unnecessary debt. Debt should always be a strategic choice, not a last resort. The nice thing about budgeting is that you don't have to be especially good at math or know how to use spreadsheets to do it right. All you need is a goal and a budgeting style that works for you.

SET YOURSELF UP FOR SUCCESS WITH ACHIEVABLE GOALS

If you had to choose a New Year's resolution you thought was reasonable between only cooking at home or limiting restaurant spending to $50 a month, you'd probably have a safer bet with option two because it's practical and quantifiable. Goals don't last long if they don't feel attainable. The key is to line up small psychological wins that will give you the momentum to keep going. For instance, maybe you need a budget because you keep finding yourself short in between paydays. Instead of promising yourself that you're going to write down every penny you spend (unlikely), you could automate with a budgeting app that tracks your spending by linking with your debit card (easier and more achievable).

Most Popular Budgeting Methods by Age

According to a WalletHub study, 27% of people 18–29 prefer budgeting apps, 39% of people aged 30–44 opt for spreadsheets, and 43% of adults 45–59 use pen and paper. Although not recommended, some 13% of adults 59+ simply keep mental tabs.

DISCOVER YOUR BUDGETING STYLE

Your budget needs to fit your lifestyle and mental bandwidth. Mental bandwidth doesn't mean your math abilities. Rather, it's how much thought and time you have to put into your budget.

First, go through your bank statements and make a list of your reoccurring expenses, like utilities, rent/mortgage, and insurance. Note due dates, which bills are set up on autopay (if any), and how much you spend on nonessentials and where. Once you have an accurate picture of your cash flow, you can start exploring budgeting techniques. Here are a few budgeting styles—just enough to give you a small peek into the vast world of money management.

The 50/30/20 Method

As one of the simpler ways of parsing out your money, the 50/30/20 budget is perfect for beginners. This method dictates that:

- **50%** of your budget should go toward **needs**.
- **30%** of your budget should go toward **wants**.
- **20%** of your budget should go toward **savings**.

A need is an unavoidable expense, like rent or mortgage payments, transportation expenses, utilities, groceries, and anything else required to survive. Wants are nice-to-haves. Streaming services, dining out, vacations, and gas station snacks are considered wants. Savings are for emergencies and goals. Ideally, you should have multiple types of savings accounts: an emergency fund for unforeseen circumstances, a regular savings account for specific goals, and a retirement account for the future.

Gamify Your Savings

See how much you can save by turning it into a game. If you're planning a vacation, draw a thermometer and fill it in every time you add to your trip fund. Visually represent freeing yourself from the chains of debt with a literal daisy chain. For every $100 you pay off, remove a link. Get a little silly to make savings fun.

The Envelope System

If you deal mostly in cash, you might find the envelope system (also known as cash-stuffing) easiest to manage. To get started, you'll label several envelopes based on spending categories that are personalized to your lifestyle. You could have envelopes for your rent payment, groceries, date nights, gym membership, and insurance. Then, you will put enough cash in each envelope to cover those expenses for a month. For example, let's say that you budget $400 a month for groceries. If you spend $100, you'll take that $100 from your groceries envelope, leaving you with $300 more that month to spend on food.

You may need to spend some time building up your envelopes. But once the system is in place, you will know that your needs are always covered as long as you can consistently replenish your envelopes and avoid tapping them for unrelated expenses.

The Zero-Based Budget

ZBB, or the zero-based budget, is best if you genuinely enjoy tracking every expense (some people do). Perhaps counterintuitively, you will have no money left over at the end of the month when using the zero-based budget. But that isn't the same as living paycheck to paycheck. Instead, the ZBB ensures that every dollar you bring in has a purpose, whether in the immediate term (like living expenses and bills) or in the future (like putting excess funds into savings or toward debt).

Zero-based budgeting is easiest if you use a spreadsheet or app (YNAB, or You Need a Budget, is a popular one). Pen and paper can also work. The most important things are diligently tracking the inflow and outflow of cash and delegating the money accordingly.

The Conscious Spending Plan

If you aren't into meticulous tracking, the conscious spending plan (CSP) might be for you. Conscious spending allows you to loosely track your expenses, emphasizing four spending categories:

- **Fixed costs** (or essential living expenses, subscriptions, and membership fees) should take up roughly **50–60%** of your post-tax monthly income.
- **Investments** should account for **10%** of your take-home pay. 401(k)s, Roth IRAs, and other investment vehicles are included in this category.

- **Savings** should take up **5–10%** of what you bring home per month. Build an emergency fund first and then sock away money for future goals, like a vacation or home improvements.
- **Guilt-free spending** is where the CSP shines. You can allocate **20–35%** of your monthly income for "fun money." Date nights, going out to eat, and hobbies fit under guilt-free spending. This leeway can help keep you on track, as long as you can avoid going overboard.

Some helpful advice: If you're bouncing back from a financial crisis or have a lot of high-interest debt, you may want to keep guilt-free spending to a minimum and beef up how much you put into the savings or fixed costs categories instead. You can reevaluate these categories as they best work for you.

BUILD AN EMERGENCY FUND

Plan for Rainy Days to Avoid a Flood

Life happens. You can't stop it, but you can plan for it. Step one is to build an emergency fund—a stockpile of funds to be used only in a crisis. Without an emergency fund, you might be forced to cover unexpected expenses like car repairs and copays with a credit card or worse—a payday loan.

Building an emergency fund might seem like an insurmountable task if you're starting from scratch. But setting small, attainable goals can help get the ball rolling. Even if it doesn't seem like much, every dollar counts, and over time, you might be surprised how much you can save with the right tactics.

Americans Struggle to Build an Emergency Fund

A survey conducted by *U.S. News & World Report* found that 42% of Americans don't have an emergency fund, and 40% can't cover an unexpected $1,000 expense.

POTENTIAL ISSUES WITHOUT AN EMERGENCY FUND

Imagine this scenario: You work a steady job, earning about $4,000 a month. This is a little more than you need to cover rent, groceries, utilities, and other living expenses. You use the overage as fun money. You've been meaning to, but you haven't yet started an emergency fund.

You wake up one morning to find that your car won't start. The repair will cost you $2,000, and, meanwhile, you can't get to work. Public transportation isn't an option where you live, and you can't afford to take an Uber every single day. You put the repair bill on your credit card. Your streak of bad luck continues when you're laid off two months later. You still have more than $1,500 left on your card for your car repair, and that balance is growing due to interest. Then, you start falling behind on rent. Eventually, your landlord tapes an eviction notice to your door.

In this scenario, an emergency fund could have covered your car repair and floated you for some time, hopefully long enough to find another job. Emergency funds aren't a failsafe (your emergency could end up costing more than what you have saved), but they do make it easier to navigate life's financial blips.

HOW MUCH SHOULD YOU SAVE FOR AN EMERGENCY FUND?

When it comes to emergency funds, the rule of thumb is to save three to six months' worth of expenses. To figure out how much this is, print out a running bank statement for a typical month. Then, organize a piece of paper into two columns. Line by line, write down which of your expenses were necessary and which were not. Be sure to note ATM withdrawals and account for cash purchases. Take your necessary expenses and multiply them by three or six. That's how much you should ideally set aside for emergencies.

FINDING ROOM IN YOUR BUDGET
FOR AN EMERGENCY FUND

Saving three to six months' worth of expenses can seem intimidating (or impossible) for consumers living paycheck to paycheck. In that case, start smaller. Any little bit set aside helps. Building an emergency fund is less about how much you can put away than it is about establishing consistent habits. If you're having trouble finding room for an emergency fund, the following tips may help.

Pay Yourself First

Out of sight, out of mind. That's the idea behind paying yourself first. If you get direct deposit, see if your employer can send your paycheck to two separate accounts, and have a small portion sent to a separate emergency fund account. It can be a challenge getting used to a smaller check, but with some adjusting, it's likely you'll stop noticing the shortage over time.

Look for Unused Subscriptions

For better or worse, we live in a subscription-based world. Subscriptions almost always auto-renew, so it's easy to lose track of what you're signed up for. Take a close look at your reoccurring drafts and nix any subscriptions you no longer use. You could even cancel all of your streaming services and replace them with free library services like Hoopla instead.

Use an App to Track Expenses

The point of saving and budgeting is not to live an utterly austere life. It's not necessary to cut out every single coffee or little splurge. What is important is to keep track of these treats—it can be easy to spent five bucks here and five bucks there, just to find out that you spent a hundred bucks without thinking. Using an app can help with this. Even for just a month, log every dollar you spend. You might be surprised where you can cut back.

Where Should You Keep Your Emergency Fund?

Don't just shove cash under your mattress. You shouldn't comingle your everyday money with your emergency fund, either. Consider parking your emergency fund in a high-yield savings account (see the "Using Windfalls Wisely" entry in this chapter). That way it can earn interest until you need to use it.

SHOULD YOU USE AN EMERGENCY FUND TO PAY DEBT?

Is debt a good reason to tap into an emergency fund? Sometimes, but it's not ideal. An emergency fund exists to help you avoid unplanned debt in the first place. Still, if you have high-interest debt or debt that is so far behind that you risk repossession or foreclosure, focus on that first. It'll be hard, if not impossible, to build an emergency fund if your debt continually grows due to runaway interest—tackling this kind of debt is sort of like shoveling while it's still snowing. Instead, take what you would put toward an emergency fund and make more than the minimum amount due on your debt payments. Once those are paid down, you can start allocating that extra money toward an emergency fund.

That doesn't mean that if you're in debt you should completely neglect an emergency fund. Open a high-yield savings account and put whatever you can into it. But focus your energy on the high-interest or secured debt first.

Also, remember that there is good debt and bad debt. Lower-interest debt or mortgage-related debt should come second to an emergency fund. You should start making extra payments on these debts only once you have three to six months of expenses saved. You could also consider allocating them to a retirement account.

USING WINDFALLS WISELY

Make That Money Work for You

Have you heard about the lottery curse? Person plays the lottery, hits it big, and finds themself broke a few years later. Interestingly, the American Bankruptcy Institute cites that about a third of lottery winners eventually file for bankruptcy. This "curse" is the result of poor planning (and maybe all those distant cousins the winner never knew they had).

Most people don't win the lottery, but it's not terribly uncommon to come into unexpected money at some point in life. Whether it's an inheritance, a big bonus at work, an insurance settlement, or something else entirely, here's a safe and practical roadmap on how to safely make it work for you.

How Much Is the Average Inheritance?

The average inheritance in the U.S. is $46,200, according to the Federal Reserve. But this number is skewed by the wealthiest families, who inherit an average of $719,000. The median may be a more realistic representation: $12,353, as per the Penn Wharton Budget Model.

GUARANTEED INVESTMENTS AND PLANNING

Unless you have an immediate need (like getting caught up on car or mortgage payments), sit on your windfall for six months before making big moves. Maybe treat yourself with something small, but afterward, park the money in a high-yield savings account or a certificate of deposit while you figure out what to do next. Both are insured by the Federal Deposit Insurance Corporation (FDIC) up to $250,000, and if used as intended, will always make money, never lose. These are extremely safe investment choices.

High-Yield Savings Account

A high-yield savings account, or HYSA, is a type of bank account that earns much more interest than a standard savings account. That's because HYSA's carry a higher annual percentage yield (APY). APY measures how much interest certain bank accounts earn. A typical savings account may carry an APY of 0.39%, while an HYSA could earn 3.99%.

The main draw to HYSAs is their flexibility, but this flexibility comes at a cost. Account holders can withdraw their money at any time. However, interest rates are variable—they go up and down with the Federal Reserve rate and overall market. When interest rates are high, savers earn more interest, but borrowing is more expensive. The inverse is also true. Lower interest rates means cheaper loans and cards, but savers earn less interest.

Certificate of Deposit

A certificate of deposit (CD) is a type of bank account that earns more than an HYSA, but your money remains locked for a certain amount of time. CD terms can run from three months to five years, but it depends on the bank or credit union issuing the CD. Credit unions call their CDs share certificates. CDs tend to have higher APYs than HYSAs.

Having your funds locked might not sound appealing, but CD interest rates are also locked. Unlike HYSAs, CDs have fixed interest rates, so you will earn the same amount of interest as the day you deposited your money. APYs tend to be higher than HYSAs. If you know for sure that you won't need your money (or a portion of your money) for a set amount of time, a CD is a great choice.

Choosing Your Advisor

Getting professional help may be wise and, depending on the amount of your windfall, might be non-negotiable. There is no threshold you must meet to hire a finance professional. Some people might be fine on their own because their financial needs are less complex and/or they have a good grasp of what to do. Others might want a professional for peace of mind, even if their windfall isn't huge. Regardless, make sure the person you hire is:

- **Properly designated:** Whoever you hire should have the proper training. Look for certified financial planners (CFPs), chartered financial analysts (CFAs), chartered financial consultants (ChFCs), or certified public accountants (CPAs).
- **Fee-only:** Fee-only financial advisors make money as a flat rate or an hourly fee. Fee-based advisors, on the other hand, can get a flat rate plus commission by selling you products.
- **A fiduciary:** A fiduciary has a legal obligation to keep their clients' best interests in mind, even if that means making less money themselves.

Getting an advisor helps put everything in order before you take the next step: using the money you've recently acquired.

USING YOUR WINDFALL

Letting your money sit and grow for at least six months will give you a cooling off period and help you avoid impulse spending. As you come up with a plan, here are some good goals to strive for. You may not achieve all of them, depending on your windfall. Generally, these are ordered from most important to least (although all are integral to a solid financial plan).

- **Create an emergency fund:** If you don't already, keep three to six months' worth of expenses in an HYSA.
- **Pay off high-interest debt:** The average return on the Standard & Poor's 500 (S&P 500) stock market index is about 10% a year. If your debt carries a rate less than 10%, consider investing instead of clearing the debt with one big payment—you'll earn more interest in the market than you'll pay on the loan. But if you have higher-interest debt, make it a priority to clear it ASAP.
- **Max out your tax-advantaged retirement and investment accounts:** Once you've made an emergency fund and paid off debt, max out your 401(k), 403(b), Roth IRA, traditional IRA, 529 plan, health savings account (HSA), and/or your flexible spending account (FSA).

Take Advantage of Employer Match

Many employers match 401(k) contributions up to a certain percentage. For instance, if your company matches up to 3% and you contribute 3%, then the total contribution will equal 6%. If you can't max out your 401(k), aim to contribute enough to take full advantage of your company's matching program.

- **Tackle other goals:** If you've been thinking about remodeling your home, a windfall might be a good way to do it. You won't have to tap into other savings, and putting more money into your home means higher property value.
- **Have fun and consider charity:** If you have enough left over, take that dream vacation you've always wanted to take. Life is short. You could also find some nonprofits that match your ideals and donate. Charitable donations are tax write-offs too.

So, while you can (and maybe should) use your windfall for some amount of frivolity, keep your financial best interests in mind.

MANAGING CREDIT DURING DIVORCE

Untangling Finances While Untangling Nuptials

Nearly a quarter of divorces (22%) stem from money issues, according to a survey conducted by the Institute for Divorce Financial Analysts (IDFA). Divorce is stressful enough, and navigating the potential impact to your credit can make things even harder. Knowing how divorce can impact your credit—and what steps to take during and after the process—might make things a little less painful.

HOW DIVORCE CAN IMPACT CREDIT

Married couples take out joint loans to buy a home, cars, and other major purchases. Some even go out of their way to co-borrow, not for the purpose of sharing assets, but to help a partner with less-than-perfect credit improve their score. Once the relationship is over, those joint ventures will need to be undone. Although getting divorced doesn't directly impact credit scores, it can still devastate the credit of one or both parties. Here are a few ways that separating finances can impact both parties' credit scores and overall credit profiles:

- Joint loans may be refinanced or closed, which will impact the length of both parties' credit history.

- Refinancing a loan requires a hard credit inquiry, and hard credit inquiries cause a slight dip in credit.
- Authorized signers will be removed from credit cards. This will impact length of credit history for the piggybacker. Once removed, the piggybacker will also have less available credit, affecting credit utilization ratio.
- Going from a dual income to a single income household will likely hurt debt-to-income ratio (DTI). Child support and alimony are also considered debt when it comes to DTI.

As you can see, divorce isn't just an emotional ordeal, but has serious financial implications as well.

PROTECTING YOUR CREDIT DURING DIVORCE

Divorce is hard for many reasons, but you don't want your credit to suffer as a result too. There are a few key things that you can do to help safeguard your credit score while going through divorce proceedings.

Pull Your Credit Reports

You'll want to order your credit reports from all three bureaus (Experian, Equifax, and TransUnion) and make note of any joint debt. Credit reports aren't standardized across the bureaus, but there are certain credit reporting codes that can help you figure out which accounts you share with your soon-to-be ex. The following table will help sort through some of those codes.

CREDIT REPORTING CODES	
CODE	**WHAT IT MEANS**
1	Individual account
2 or J	Joint account
3 or A	Authorized user
5 or C	Cosigner
7 or M	Indicates an account with a cosigner who is someone other than a spouse
T	Terminated, or no longer responsible for account
W	Business or commercial account
X	Deceased
Z	Consumer deleted

It's essential to order and examine your credit reports before, during, and after divorce. Before proceedings, your credit reports will let you know which loans and cards you hold jointly and that will need to be untangled. During and after the divorce, continue checking your reports to ensure that these accounts were separated properly.

Continue Paying Jointly Owned Debts

Even if you and your spouse are not on speaking terms, it's essential that you both continue paying joint debts. If your spouse refuses to pay their portion, consider picking up the slack (you can address this later during divorce proceedings). Missed payments, even ones you share, have a huge impact. At 35%, payment history makes up the lion's share of a FICO Score.

Remove Your Ex As an Authorized User

An authorized signer has the privilege of racking up debt, but they have no obligation to pay it. Remove your ex as an authorized user so they can't accrue debt in your name. Remove yourself as an authorized user from their cards too, if applicable.

Refinance Co-borrowed Loans

Some couples wait until after the divorce decree to refinance any co-borrowed loans, but ripping off the Band-Aid now can make things smoother later—that is, if you both can amicably agree on who owes what. Typically, the only way to remove a co-borrower from a loan is to refinance it into just one of the borrowers' names.

Freeze Your Credit

Lock down your credit to prevent anyone other than yourself from applying for any new loans or cards. For more information, see the "Credit Freezes and Fraud Alerts" entry in Chapter 9.

HOW TO PROTECT YOUR CREDIT AFTER DIVORCE

Your divorce decree does not override your loan agreements. Just because a judge orders your ex to keep up with their side on a jointly held mortgage doesn't guarantee that your ex will do so. Your lender cares about who is responsible for the loan according to your loan or card contract, regardless of relationship status. The following are all ways to shield your credit after your marriage ends.

Confirm Joint Loans Have Been Addressed

Make sure all joint loans have been refinanced into one of your names after the divorce is final. The judge may have also ordered you to sell jointly owned assets and split the proceeds.

What Happens with the House?

If your mortgage includes both you and your ex-spouse, the judge will typically order one of three things:

- That the house be refinanced in just one of the couple's names
- That the house be sold and the proceeds be split
- That one half of the couple may need to "buy out" their ex by paying them their share of the remaining equity, if they want to keep the house

Keep Pulling Your Credit Reports

It can take months to finalize a divorce. As the dust settles, continue monitoring your credit reports to spot any issues that may still need addressing.

Change Passwords

Don't forget to update your credentials for your online banking portals and mobile apps. You should be the only one with access to accounts that are held only in your name.

Update Your Budget

Surviving on your own financially can be a struggle if you're coming from a dual income household. Any major life change, whether it be marriage, pregnancy, or divorce, calls for a budget review. Retool your budget to account for an altered cash flow. For budget tips, see the entry "Maintain a Budget" earlier in this chapter.

Build Individual Credit History

Keep your individual accounts open and consider getting a new card or loan. If you don't qualify for a traditional lending product, you could get a secured credit card or credit-builder loan to start.

HANDLING CREDIT AFTER THE LOSS OF A SPOUSE

A Helping Hand During the Hardest Time

The death of a spouse is an unimaginable loss, but unfortunately, grief doesn't stop the bills. Understanding what debt you're ultimately responsible for will help you protect your credit score and avoid spending money on bills you aren't required to pay.

PROTECTING YOUR DECEASED SPOUSE'S IDENTITY

Protecting your deceased spouse's identity is a necessary task. If an identity thief opens up credit in your spouse's name (called ghosting), whatever debt they accrue will be the responsibility of your spouse's estate until you can prove that your spouse's identity was stolen. Ghosting can lengthen probate. Probate is a legal process that is typically required after someone dies. Here, the executor of estate will pay off any applicable debt left behind by the deceased (using the deceased's assets) and then distribute the remaining assets to heirs and beneficiaries. An executor of estate is someone (a person usually named in the deceased's will) who is deemed legally responsible to tie up the deceased's financial affairs. If there was no will, then the court may appoint an administrator (usually the deceased's spouse or adult children) to handle these tasks. You could also be held responsible for this fraudulent debt if you live in a community property state. After your spouse dies, you should immediately notify the credit bureaus and your spouse's creditors. They will most likely ask for proof of death, so plan ahead and order several death certificates to send. The credit bureaus will list your spouse as deceased on their credit report, which should stop fraudsters from using your spouse's file to rack up debt.

Also notify the Social Security Administration. The funeral home normally handles this step, but it doesn't hurt to be thorough. During the phone call, you'll learn more about any benefits you could be entitled to.

YOUR DEBT-RELATED RESPONSIBILITIES

Whether or not you have to pay your deceased spouse's debt depends on many factors, like who legally owns the debt, whether you cosigned, where you live, and whether your spouse has an estate. Estate law is complicated, and it varies significantly by state. The information in this book will get you started, but it's best to speak with an estate attorney. Here are some of the rules of thumb that apply to debt after someone dies.

Joint and Cosigned

You are responsible for debt in which you're listed as the co-borrower or cosigner. The debt will be transferred or refinanced in your name only, and you are required to continue making payments.

Married couples often co-borrow to buy a house or a car. What happens to those physical assets if you can't pay? If you do nothing, the lender will repossess the car or foreclose on the house. This will ruin your credit. Instead, contact the lender and ask for options. They may be able to modify the loan to make it easier to manage. If they can't, then consider selling the asset yourself and using the proceeds to pay as much of the loan as you can. You'll have to pay the difference, if there is one. You could also give the asset back to the lender. This is called a voluntary repossession if the asset is a car, and a deed in lieu of foreclosure if it's a house. These actions also hurt your credit, but less so than if the repossession or foreclosure was involuntary.

Debt Accrued by Your Spouse During Marriage

In community property states, most debt accrued during the marriage is the responsibility of both parties, no matter whose name is on the debt. Most states are not community property states, but you'll have to research your state specifically for more information. But even if you live in a community property state, exceptions exist. Prenuptial agreements supersede community property laws, for instance. If a prenup states that one party will be responsible for debt incurred during marriage, then that is the case—regardless of community property laws.

Debt Covered by the Doctrine of Necessaries

Some states follow the doctrine of necessaries. The doctrine of necessaries is a very old law that was originally created to ensure that husbands took care of their wife's necessary needs after death (like food, shelter, and medical care). Today, some states still follow the doctrine of necessaries (but in a gender-neutral way). In these cases, a spouse could be responsible for their deceased spouse's medical bills related to their final illness and/or nursing home care. Whether the doctrine of necessaries applies depends on whether the remaining spouse has the means to pay for said bills and how strictly their state follows the doctrine, if at all.

The Doctrine of Necessaries and Debt Collectors

Some debt collectors will cite the doctrine of necessaries when attempting to collect debt. However, due to the law's complexity, it's possible that the doctrine doesn't apply to you. If a debt collector mentions the doctrine of necessaries, consult with an attorney before paying.

UNDERSTANDING WHAT DEBTS YOU'RE NOT RESPONSIBLE FOR

Under the Fair Debt Collection Practices Act, debt collectors can call you to ask about your spouse's death, but they cannot demand payment for debt you aren't legally responsible for. Generally, you won't have to pay debt in your spouse's name only, unless you live in a community property state.

When someone dies, their debt is paid out of their estate, or the collection of assets they leave behind. The deceased's personal representative is responsible for liquidating assets and paying the deceased's debts. Anything left over goes to the deceased's beneficiaries. If there's any unresolved debt, the creditor will write it off as a loss.

Chapter 7

Credit Cards

Credit cards can be one of the best tools in your personal finance toolkit, but only if you use them strategically. Using credit cards, you can borrow money for free and earn points, cashback, or miles. You can improve your credit score with on-time payments. Plus, in a lot of ways, credit cards offer more flexibility than loans. With just one approval, you can borrow as often as you'd like, assuming you have the credit available.

At the same time, credit cards have caused many issues for those who don't use them responsibly. If you don't truly understand how credit cards really work before you tap, type, or swipe, you could find yourself ensnared in the trap of runaway compounding interest. This chapter aims to help you sidestep the potential issues with cards and instead reap the rewards that can follow when you use them strategically, intentionally, and with caution.

CREDIT CARD BASICS

An Introduction to the World of Plastic

In general, all credit cards work the same way. They're a form of revolving debt with a set spending (or credit) limit. Using the card reduces the amount of credit the borrower has left to spend, and credit is replenished when the cardholder makes payments. Credit limits are determined by the card issuer. The better the cardholder's credit, the higher the credit limit they'll qualify for. But that's where the similarities stop. How a credit card works at a more granular level depends on the type of card and how the cardholder uses it.

DIFFERENT TYPES OF CREDIT CARDS

Choosing a credit card can be confusing due to the sheer number of options out there. To get the most bang for their buck, consumers should choose a credit card that best aligns with their needs, goals, and spending habits. Here are some options:

- **Standard credit cards:** A standard credit card comes with few to no perks but also with fewer fees and lower rates than rewards credit cards.
- **Rewards credit cards:** Cardholders can earn points, cashback, or airline miles by using a rewards credit card.
- **Balance transfer credit cards:** These types of credit cards are designed to absorb debt from another card or cards.

- **Student credit cards:** Some issuers offer credit cards to college students, specifically to help them establish a credit history. Student credit cards have lower limits and lower interest rates than standard cards.
- **Secured credit cards:** Secured credit cards require a cash deposit, and this deposit serves as the card's spending limit. Bad- and thin-credit borrowers commonly use secured cards to build a positive payment history.
- **Co-branded credit cards:** Sometimes, card issuers and other companies work together to offer a co-branded card. The Delta SkyMiles® Gold American Express Card, for example, is a co-branded card between American Express and Delta Air Lines. By using the card, the cardholder racks up rewards that can be redeemed with the card's partner (in this case, Delta Air Lines).
- **Store credit cards:** A store credit card only works at the store that offers it. Store cards are usually only a good idea if you're a frequent shopper at the store in question, can earn some sort of reward by using it regularly, and can pay off your balance in full each month. Store cards tend to have higher interest rates than most other types of credit cards.

Compounding Interest at Work

Imagine a cardholder named Hazel. She used her card to buy a $2,500 Jet Ski. Her credit card annual percentage rate (APR) is 23%, with a minimum monthly payment of $75. If Hazel only pays the minimum, she'll pay about $3,800 in interest, turning a $2,500 Jet Ski into a $6,300+ Jet Ski.

TYPES OF CREDIT CARD APRS

Credit card APRs don't work the same as loan APRs. Both measure the cost of borrowing over one year, but loan APRs include interest and fees. Credit card APRs, on the other hand, only represent a card's interest rate. Fees are shown separately. Plus, unlike a loan, credit card issuers charge different rates on the same card, depending on what the card was used for. If a cardholder used their card to buy groceries and also to get a cash advance, then their total credit card balance will have two different APRs. The groceries would carry the card's purchase APR, while the cash advance would carry the card's cash advance APR. The following are some different kinds of APRs you may encounter:

- **Purchase APRs** apply to standard purchases. Of all the APRs on a credit card, a purchase APR is usually the lowest.
- **Cash advance APRs** apply to cash advances. A cash advance allows borrowers to use their card to access cash from ATMs and banks. Cash advance APRs are generally high.
- **Balance transfer APRs** apply to balance transfers. A balance transfer allows a cardholder to shift one or more credit card balances to another card, hopefully one with a lower interest rate. Standard and rewards credit cards usually have a high balance transfer APR. Balance transfer cards typically offer 0% APR for a certain amount of time.
- **Penalty APRs** can apply as a result of a few different actions. If a cardholder doesn't pay at least the minimum amount due by their due date, then their card issuer might apply a penalty APR to replace their purchase APR. Card issuers typically don't charge penalty APRs until the cardholder is more than sixty

days late. Federal law also states that issuers must notify the cardholder at least forty-five days in advance before applying a penalty APR.

- **Introductory APRs** are a way for issuers to attract business by offering new cardholders a period of low to no interest for a limited time—commonly between six and twenty-one months, according to Experian. Any balance left over after the intro APR period is over is subject to the card's standard purchase APR.

- **Promotional APRs** are similar to introductory APRs, but they usually apply to existing cardholders rather than to new cards. An example of a promotional APR could be 0% interest for twelve months on purchases over $400. After the twelve months are over, any remaining balance may be subject to the card's standard purchase APR, or the standard APR may be backdated to the day of the original purchase. The latter is technically deferred interest, which is further discussed in this chapter under the entry "Deferred Interest versus 0% Intro APR."

These many types of APRs distinguish between cards and loans, with typical credit card APRs being much more involved compared to loans.

CREDIT CARD BEST PRACTICES

Using Credit Cards to Support Your Score

Although it's a popular misconception, carrying a credit card balance to build credit history is not a good idea. Doing so can help a borrower build a positive payment history, but it's an incredibly expensive way to achieve your goal. Credit card interest compounds daily. So how should borrowers use a credit card to build their score?

CREDIT CARD BEST PRACTICES

Using a credit card like a pro requires intent and strategy. Every piece of guidance in the following section impacts a borrower's credit score, either directly or indirectly. Borrowers should see their scores flourish over time if they follow these rules of thumb.

Pay On Time, Every Time

In a perfect world, cardholders would pay their monthly credit card bills in full by the end of each billing cycle to avoid paying interest. But the world isn't perfect, and not all cardholders can do that. Whether a cardholder is carrying a balance or not, they should always pay at least the minimum amount due by the time it's due. Paying on time is essential for a positive payment history, and payment history makes up 35% of a FICO Score (a popular brand of credit score).

Consider Balances Across All Cards and Lines of Credit

Credit utilization is a huge driver of FICO's amounts-owed credit scoring factor. As a reminder, amounts owed makes up 30% of a FICO Score and measures how much revolving credit a borrower is using compared to how much revolving credit they have available to them. Many lenders have a credit utilization cutoff of 30%, but lower is better. Credit utilization doesn't just measure the balance on a single card, so borrowers should consider how much revolving debt they have across all of their cards and lines of credit.

Consider Balances Across All Forms of Debt

A borrower's total level of revolving and installment debt affects the amounts-owed category (just not as much as credit utilization does, which only considers revolving debt). Further, total debt determines debt-to-income ratio. If a lender sees that the borrower has an outsized level of debt compared to their income, the lender will hesitate to extend credit. Debt-to-income ratio is not a credit scoring factor, but it is something that lenders evaluate when reviewing credit reports.

No Impulse Purchasing

This has been mentioned before, but it's worth mentioning again: The key to using a credit card to build and improve your score is only using it for certain purchases and to have a payoff plan. If you wouldn't use your debit card to buy an item because the money isn't currently available, then it's probably best not to put it on your credit card, either. Counting chickens before they hatch—or assuming the funds will be available by the time your credit card bill comes due—is a common way borrowers get caught in the debt cycle.

Use the Card Regularly

Most credit card issuers will deactivate a credit card after it's been dormant for a certain amount of time, and each credit card issuer makes its own timeline guidelines. Generally, though, issuers usually deactivate a card if it hasn't been used in six months or several years. If an issuer closes a card, this can affect credit utilization, since the borrower will have less credit available to use. And if the closed card is one of the borrower's oldest, they should expect a drop in the length of their credit history, a factor that makes up 15% of a FICO Score.

Apply Sparingly

New credit only accounts for 10% of a FICO Score, but every little financial move makes a difference. We went over the fourteen- and forty-five-day rate shopping window in Chapter 2, but it's important to note **that the rate shopping window does not apply to credit cards, only to certain loans, like auto loans and mortgages**. When shopping for a new credit card or line of credit, borrowers should prequalify for the cards they're considering before choosing to apply for a certain card. Prequalification only requires a soft credit hit and will have no impact on FICO's "new credit" scoring factor.

UNOFFICIAL CREDIT CARD SECRETS

The credit card "rules" that follow are unwritten guidelines based on the general experience of applicants and cardholders. Knowing these can help you avoid pursuing a card and taking a hard credit hit for something that you won't qualify for based on your current credit card portfolio. Unofficially, keep in mind:

- **American Express's 1/5 rule:** American Express will not approve two credit card applications submitted within the same five days. This only applies to credit cards, not charge cards.
- **American Express's 2/90 rule:** American Express will not approve an applicant for two credit cards within the same ninety-day period.
- **Chase's 5/24 rule:** Chase will not approve an applicant for a new credit card if they have opened five or more accounts with any bank within the last twenty-four months.
- **Bank of America's 2/3/4 rule:** Bank of America will only approve two new cards within a thirty-day window, three new cards within twelve months, and four cards within twenty-four months. This only applies to Bank of America credit cards. If the applicant has been approved for three cards in a thirty-day time period and one of those was with a different bank, this rule wouldn't apply.
- **Bank of America's 3/12 rule:** Unless the applicant has a Bank of America checking account with a decent balance ($2,500 to $5,000, for example), the bank will not approve a new card if the applicant has opened three or more cards over the last twelve months.

Though you likely shouldn't be opening many credit cards at the same time, you'll definitely want to keep this information in mind when you are applying to cards.

Credit Cards Aren't the Same As Charge Cards

The terms are often used interchangeably, but credit cards and charge cards aren't the same. Charge cards (which are uncommon) require the borrower to pay their balance in full at each billing cycle, and they don't have a preset spending limit.

CREDIT CARD FEES

The Price of Plastic, Not Fantastic

Assuming the borrower pays of their balance in full each month, credit cards are a great way to borrow money without accruing interest, but that doesn't necessarily mean that the money was free. Almost every credit card carries at least one fee. Not all fees apply on every card or in every situation, but knowing about these fees and where to find them in a credit card agreement will help you understand how much it truly costs to swipe or tap.

WHICH ISSUERS CHARGE THE HIGHEST FEES?

Bigger isn't always better. Every six months, the Consumer Financial Protection Bureau conducts the Terms of Credit Card Plans survey to inform consumers about credit card APRs (annual percentage rates) and rate trends. Based on those findings, credit cards issued by large banks are typically more expensive than those from smaller banks and credit unions. Data from over 150 financial institutions showed that:

- Credit cards from larger institutions were three times more likely to charge an annual fee, compared to small banks and credit unions. A little over a quarter of the big banks studied (27%) charged an annual fee. In comparison, only 9.5% of small banks and credit unions charged an annual credit card fee.

- Annual credit card fees charged by large banks were 67% higher than those at small institutions. The biggest banks charged an annual credit card fee of $157, while smaller issuers charged $94, on average.
- Credit cards from the top twenty-five largest banks carried significantly higher APRs than cards issued by small banks and credit unions. Whether the borrower had excellent or bad credit, APRs from these large banks were 8–10% higher.

Where to Check for Credit Card Fees

Named after legislator Charles Schumer, the Schumer Box is a legally required disclosure that must be included with credit card offers and card statements. The Schumer Box displays the different APRs, fees, and the interest rate grace periods that apply to the card. If you're comparing cards, the Schumer Box is an excellent place to start.

COMMON CREDIT CARD FEES

Interest isn't the only fee that can accompany a credit card. Credit cards can come with multiple fees. When a credit card issuer charges a fee, it adds that fee to the card's balance, where it has the potential to grow interest. Here are some common credit card fees.

Annual Fee

Some card issuers charge cardholders a fee each year for nothing other than having the card. Typical annual fees range from $95 to more than $695, but they vary by credit card. In fact, most people skip annual fees altogether, according to the Federal Reserve Bank of Atlanta. It conducted a survey and found that only about one in five cardholders pay an annual credit fee.

When a credit card charges an annual fee, it's usually for one of two reasons. First, most rewards cards come with an annual fee. If the cardholder spends enough, these rewards could offset the cost of the fee. Second, subprime credit cards (credit cards made for those with bad credit) also often charge annual fees. No matter if it's a loan, card, or another way of borrowing, the worse a borrower's credit, the more likely they are to pay fees.

If you're considering a card with an annual fee, make sure that the fee will be worth it over the long haul. Closing an old account can hurt your credit score, so you'll have to choose between continuing to pay the fee year over year or closing the credit card and taking a possible hit to your credit. It can be easy to lose sight of this if the rewards seem extra sweet or if the issuer is waiving its annual fee for the first year.

Late and Returned Payment Fees

Credit card issuers usually charge a fee if the cardholder doesn't pay at least the minimum amount by the due date. Some cards come with a grace period that allows for a few extra days before a fee applies. Returned payments also typically trigger a fee.

Ask and You Might Receive

Don't be afraid to ask your credit card issuer for lower rates and fees. According to a LendingTree survey, 83% of cardholders who asked for a lower interest rate got one. Card issuers also reduced or waived annual fees for a whopping 95% of cardholders who asked.

Foreign Transaction Fee

On cards that have them, a foreign transaction fee applies if the cardholder uses their card to pay for a purchase that is in a non-U.S. currency, or if the charge is made through an international bank (shopping online with an overseas store, for instance). Typical foreign transaction fees are 1–3% of the total transaction.

Cash Advance Fee

Typically, cash advance fees are 3–5% of the total advance amount. Cash advance fees can apply on more than just cash withdrawals. Using your card to pay a loan or transfer money through Venmo could lead to a cash advance fee.

Authorized User Fee

Credit card companies may charge a fee for adding an authorized user to an account. These fees can be substantial, sometimes several hundred dollars. These fees are also typically charged for every year the authorized user is listed on the account.

Balance Transfer Fee

Most credit cards charge a balance transfer fee of 3–5% of the total amount being transferred. If the cardholder is transferring a balance from more than one card, each transfer gets its own balance transfer fee.

DEFERRED INTEREST VERSUS 0% INTRO APR

Know the Difference to Avoid a Pricey Surprise

No money down and no interest for twelve months—sounds like a pretty great deal, right? It can be, but it depends on whether the offer is truly 0% interest or if the interest is deferred. With a 0% APR (annual percentage rate) intro period, the borrower won't pay any interest for a certain amount of time, regardless of any leftover balance when the intro period ends. With deferred interest, the borrower could be on the hook for a massive amount of interest if they don't get their balance paid in full before a certain period. Both options sound similar, and unless you read the small print, they are often advertised the same.

WHAT IS DEFERRED INTEREST?

Deferred interest (also sometimes called special financing) comes with a promotional period. During the promotional period, the borrower won't pay interest. Interest still accrues, but it technically isn't due—yet. If the borrower pays their balance in full by the end of their promotional period, the card issuer or lender will waive any interest. If there's a balance left, the interest is backdated to the date of the original purchase and added to the borrower's overall balance, where it will continue to accrue interest. You're more likely to find deferred interest on store credit cards, specialized credit cards meant for a specific purpose (like medical bills), and in-house installment loans.

Prepare to Pay More Than Minimum

Monthly statements on deferred interest show two amounts due. One is the minimum you can pay and still be considered current. The other is the suggested amount due, which is what you need to make to pay your balance by the end of the promo period.

WHAT IS 0% INTRO APR?

A 0% intro APR credit card comes with an introductory period. An introductory period is a more consumer-friendly version of a promotional period. Like a promo period, the borrower has a predetermined length of time to pay off their debt. But unlike a promo period, interest isn't backdated if there is a leftover balance once the intro period ends. Instead, interest will apply to the balance moving forward and isn't backdated. You can find 0% intro APR cards with most major credit card issuers, but it usually takes excellent credit to qualify.

Differences Outlined in a Chart

It can be hard to tell the difference between 0% intro APR and deferred interest. The following table lays everything out for you.

DEFERRED INTEREST AND 0% APR AT A GLANCE		
FEATURE	DEFERRED INTEREST	0% INTRO APR
What it means	No interest if the balance is paid by the end of the promo period	No interest during intro period, even if a balance is left at the end
What happens if a balance is left at the end	Interest is backdated to the original charge	Interest begins to accrue on the remaining balance
Credit required	May qualify with fair credit	Need at least good credit, usually excellent
Often applies to ...	Store cards, in-store financing, and specialized cards for medical/vet/dentist financing	0% intro APR cards offered by major banks and card issuers
What to look for in fine print	No interest if paid in full within the disclosed number of months	0% APR for the disclosed number of months
Biggest risk	A massive chunk of interest added to debt if the borrower can't pay in full by the end of the promo period	Borrower may be tempted to overspend during the intro period

DEFERRED INTEREST AND 0% INTRO APR IN ACTION

Deferred interest isn't always a bad idea. If the borrower has an iron-clad payoff plan that ensures that they will have absolutely no debt left by the end of their promo period (not even a dollar), then no interest will apply. But deferred interest is no doubt risky, as interest still looms in the background. A 0% APR card is the safer choice, because interest simply doesn't accrue during the intro period.

To put this into perspective, imagine two borrowers who are each buying a $3,000 computer. One borrower (Sam) used a store card with deferred interest for his purchase. The other (Michelle) used a 0% APR intro credit card. Both Sam and Michelle needed to pay off their computers in six months in order to skip interest. This required a monthly payment of at least $500. Both cards carry a 24.99% APR when interest does apply. Unfortunately, neither Sam nor Michelle were able to pay their final $500 bill at the end of their respective promo and intro periods. Here's what happened next.

Sam's Experience with Deferred Interest

Since Sam could not pay off his computer by the end of his six-month promotional period, the interest that was accruing in the background during the promo period was added to his $500 balance. To figure out how much deferred interest to add, Sam's card issuer calculated his monthly interest rate by dividing his APR by twelve. So, 24.99% ÷ 12 = 2.08%.

Then, it took that monthly interest rate, applied it to each month's balance, and added what accrued to the remaining $500 balance.

MONTH	BEGINNING BALANCE	MONTHLY INTEREST
1	$3,000	$62.40
2	$2,500	$52.00
3	$2,000	$41.60
4	$1,500	$31.20
5	$1,000	$20.80
6	$500	$10.40

At the end of the promo period, Sam's card issuer added $218.40 in deferred interest charges to his $500 balance. Instead of owing $500, he now owes $718.40 at 24.99% APR.

Michelle's Experience with a 0% APR Intro Credit Card

Michelle's situation is much simpler (and cheaper) than Sam's. Although she also had $500 left at the end of her six-month intro period, interest was not backdated and added to her remaining balance because interest never accrued in the first place. Instead, she will owe $500 at 24.99% APR.

CREDIT CARD INCENTIVES

Choosing Between Travel, Rewards, and Cashback Cards

Credit card incentives won't make you rich, but they are icing on the cake. Minus annual fees, credit card companies could actually end up paying you for using their card via incentives (assuming you skip interest by paying your balance in full each billing cycle). There are so many different types of rewards that these cards offer, and picking what reward(s) you want through your credit is a decision only you can make.

DIFFERENT TYPES OF REWARDS CARDS

Some people take out dozens of rewards cards and cycle through them strategically to earn the most incentives. This is called churning, and it's only recommended for experienced, disciplined borrowers. Churning also takes a lot of time and planning, and repeatedly opening and closing accounts can damage credit scores. If you're like most people, it's better to choose one or two rewards cards with incentives that align best with your goals.

While reviewing your options, know that it usually takes a good to excellent credit score to qualify for a rewards credit card. This equates to a score of 670+ if using FICO Scores (which credit card issuers almost always do).

Cashback Credit Cards

A cashback credit card gives cardholders back a percentage of what they spend, usually by statement credits, direct deposits, or gift cards. Some cashback cards work as a flat rate: For every dollar spent, the cardholder will earn some previously disclosed percentage back. Others offer different cashback rates based on spending categories. For instance, the cardholder might earn at least 1% on every purchase, but 2% on dining. Sometimes, category rates rotate monthly or quarterly.

Extra Incentives, Extra Cost

Generally, rewards cards have higher annual fees—often close to $1,000 with top-tier cards. Make sure that you can break even with incentives based on your current spending habits.

Travel Credit Cards

Generally, travel credit cards can be broken down into two categories: flexible and co-branded. Travel cards often split spending into categories, with certain types of spending earning higher rewards, not unlike cashback cards. Travel cards also tend to come with travel-specific perks, like airport lounge access or TSA PreCheck.

Flexible Travel Credit Cards

Flexible travel credit cards allow cardholders to earn points that can be redeemed for flights and/or hotel stays. They don't have to book with a specific airline or hotel chain (although they might get better value if they do, depending on possible card partnerships).

The cardholder simply logs into their online account and redeems their points toward any eligible flight or stay. Hence the term "flexible" travel credit cards.

Co-branded Travel Credit Cards

Instead of points, co-branded travel cards usually earn miles that can only be redeemed with specific airlines or hotel chains. In this context, miles aren't literal; it's just how the card issuer measures its incentive. A flight from Tampa to Detroit could cost 15,000 miles, although the destinations are only a little over 1,000 miles apart.

Along with different spending categories, cardholders typically earn extra miles for spending with the airline the card is branded with or bonus flight credits for spending a certain amount each year. Co-branded travel credit cards are best for those who are loyal to a specific airline or chain.

Exchanging Miles for Money

Some co-branded cards let you convert miles into dollars. However, the exchange rate is usually pretty low—one mile might be worth a penny. Co-branded card issuers incentivize cardholders to spend with the brand. To them, converting miles to dollars defeats this purpose.

CREDIT CARD SIGN-UP BONUSES

Also known as a welcome offer, a credit card sign-up bonus is an incentive that card issuers use to encourage borrowers to apply. Sign-up bonuses can be very generous, sometimes allowing the cardholder to earn thousands of dollars, points, or miles in a short amount of time. Churners tend to focus on sign-up bonuses, targeting and cycling through the cards with the best offers.

Common Sign-Up Bonus Rules

The term "sign-up bonus" can make it sound like the bonus is guaranteed as long as the borrower is approved. This isn't the case. Cardholders usually must meet a strict set of rules after they get the card to qualify for the bonus. Firstly, you must meet a minimum spend requirement (MSR). Almost every sign-up bonus has an MSR. This is a preset amount that the cardholder must charge within a certain amount of time to qualify. For instance, the sign-up bonus might require the cardholder to charge $3,000 within the first three months. Without an MSR, what's stopping the new cardholder from collecting their bonus and immediately cancelling the card? That wouldn't do the issuer any good.

Then, you must remember that not all spending counts toward earning a sign-up bonus. Cash advances, balance transfers, and, with some issuers, gift card purchases, don't count toward the MSR. The same goes for spending that the issuer considers "cash equivalent," like gambling or buying crypto.

Finally, know that issuers typically limit how many sign-up bonuses someone can get. For instance, you might only qualify for one bonus even if you sign up for multiple cards, if those cards are within the same "family" of cards or are from the same issuer.

Common Traps and Best Practices

As lucrative as welcome bonuses can be, they can also cause problems if the cardholder doesn't have a strategy when applying.

The following are some tips for you to use credit cards as best you can:

- **Don't overspend just to earn a bonus.** Spending more than you can afford (or on things you don't need) just to get a welcome bonus isn't wise. Have a plan on how you'll meet the offer's MSR before applying. Time your application around a pre-planned, big-ticket item. Or you could use the card for all of your essentials (like groceries) until you meet the MSR. Just be sure that you can still pay your balance in full each billing cycle to avoid snowballing interest charges.
- **Don't apply for a card just for the welcome bonus.** Welcome bonuses are great, but they're a one-time benefit. The card should also have an acceptable interest rate (if you plan on carrying a balance, a practice we don't recommend) and/or other benefits that you're interested in.
- **Read the fine print.** You have one shot to earn your welcome bonus. If you don't meet the issuer's MSR, there are no do-overs. Know what purchases qualify for the welcome bonus and which don't, how long you have to earn the welcome bonus, and other terms and conditions.
- **Keep the card for at least a year.** Some issuers will take back their welcome offer if you cancel the card within the first year.

Remembering these tips will help you make the best decisions related to getting a new card.

CREDIT CARD CASH ADVANCES

Are They Really Worth It?

Most major credit cards let you withdraw cash from ATMs, at banks, or through special checks. This is called a cash advance. Although cash advances can be a lifesaver in emergencies, they aren't something cardholders should do often thanks to high interest and fees.

HOW CREDIT CARD CASH ADVANCES WORK

When a cardholder takes a cash advance, they're getting a loan from their credit card. These loans are usually limited to a certain percentage of the card's total credit limit. For instance, if you have a $10,000 credit limit and your issuer allows you to access 20% as a cash advance, you'd be able to take out $2,000. Perhaps the most significant benefit to cash advances is that they don't require a separate credit check. Because you are already approved for the card, you are already approved for the cash advance (assuming your card allows them).

CASH ADVANCES DIFFER FROM STANDARD CHARGES

Cash advances sound pretty sweet, but in reality they're a bit of a sour deal (most credit products designed for emergencies usually are). The following are all reasons that they aren't as great as they seem.

Higher Rates and Extra Fees

As discussed in the "Credit Card Fees" entry in this chapter, each credit card function typically carries its own APR. For cash advances, this APR is generally 5–10% higher than a standard charge. Cash advances also come with a separate up-front cash advance fee—usually 3–5% of the amount the cardholder is withdrawing. This fee is tacked onto the credit card's balance.

No Grace Period on Interest

Credit cards have a built-in grace period for standard charges. As long as the cardholder pays their card off before the end of their billing cycle, interest will not apply. This is not the case with cash advances. Instead, interest begins accruing from the moment the cardholder takes the advance.

Not All Cash Advances Actually Advance Cash

If you see an unexplained cash advance on your billing statement, it could be because of a different transaction. Using your card for sports betting and gambling, gift cards, peer-to-peer money transfers (like Cash App), and buying crypto can all be considered cash equivalents that come with a cash advance fee.

No Rewards, Points, or Miles

Cash advances do not help cardholders earn rewards, points, or miles. Those benefits are reserved for standard charges. That means the borrower is not only paying more fees and higher interest, but they can't leverage this more expensive form of borrowing to earn bonuses.

HOW CASH ADVANCES IMPACT CREDIT

Credit card cash advances don't impact credit scores any differently than a standard charge. Cash advances and regular charges look the same on a credit report, and both are considered part of a borrower's credit utilization ratio. Credit utilization ratio measures how much credit a borrower has available compared to how much they are actually using. A cash advance eats up more of the borrower's available credit, leading to an increase in their credit utilization ratio. Generally, the lower a borrower's credit utilization ratio, the better, with 1–7% being ideal. Credit utilization ratio is a significant contributor to FICO's amounts-owed credit scoring factor. This makes up 30% of a FICO Score.

The biggest risk associated with credit card cash advances isn't the credit score impact, it's the cycle of debt that they can trigger. Namely, due to how credit card payments are applied. When a borrower makes the minimum payment due, the issuer can decide how to apply the payment. Usually, they prioritize fees, then interest from lowest to highest rate, and then principal. If you plan on taking a cash advance, also plan on paying more than your minimum amount due to avoid the higher APR on a cash advance.

The Credit Card Act of 2009 states that card issuers must apply excess payments to balances with the highest APR first. This means that, when a cardholder makes more than the minimum payment, the overage will likely go toward the cash advance balance since it has a higher APR than a standard charge. If the cardholder isn't prepared to make more than the minimum payment, that cash advance could sit for a long time, accruing interest as other interest and fees take precedence unless more than the minimum is paid.

BALANCE TRANSFERS

Strategically Reducing the Amount of Interest You'll Pay

It might not feel like it, but borrowers who are carrying a lot of high-interest credit card debt have options. One of those options is balance transfer credit cards. A balance transfer card is similar to a debt consolidation loan. The borrower will transfer their current credit card debt (whether it's on one card or spread across several) onto a single balance transfer card.

HOW BALANCE TRANSFER CREDIT CARDS WORK

A balance transfer credit card is designed to absorb credit card debt the borrower carries on other cards. If done right, a balance transfer can help a borrower pay significantly less credit card interest, oftentimes none. Balance transfer cards come with a low- or no-interest introductory period. Lengths vary by issuer, but typical introductory periods run from six to twenty-one months. If the borrower pays off their card during this introductory period, then they will either pay no interest or low interest on their debt—whatever the card's introductory APR is.

Balance transfer cards do have some drawbacks. For one, any balance remaining after the intro period will be subject to the card's standard purchase APR (which may not be competitive compared to traditional credit cards). Also, balance transfer cards usually charge a balance transfer fee between 3–5% of the balance being transferred. So, if you were transferring a $10,000 balance onto a card with a 5% balance transfer fee, the balance transfer will cost $500, which will be rolled into your credit card balance. That balance transfer fee will likely be far less than what you'd pay in interest, but it's still something to consider, especially if you plan on transferring balances more than once.

Rate Surfing: Think Twice Before Hanging Ten

Rate surfers perpetually shift credit card debt from one balance transfer card to another. On paper, this helps them avoid paying interest indefinitely. But what happens if they don't qualify for another 0% interest balance transfer card when their current intro period ends? In that case, they'll be saddled with a lot of high-interest credit card debt.

HOW A BALANCE TRANSFER IMPACTS CREDIT

Based on Consumer Financial Protection Bureau data, the vast majority of borrowers who use balance transfer cards have strong credit, as more than 98% of balance transfers are conducted by borrowers with prime credit scores or higher (660+). Most card issuers require at least good credit to qualify for a balance transfer card. When speaking to credit score impact, balance transfers can affect different borrowers in different ways. It depends on the borrower's current credit score, how much debt they have, and other factors. Generally, though, borrowers can expect the following after a balance transfer:

Potential Negative Impacts
- **A small initial credit score dip due to the hard credit inquiry the credit issuer will run at the time of application.** Hard credit inquiries tend to only drop scores down by five points or less, and only for a year (although it will show on a credit report for two years).
- **A decrease in score due to opening a new card.** New cards and loans drop the average age of a borrower's length of credit history (which makes up 15% of a FICO Score). This is especially true if the borrower closes their old card(s) after the balance transfer.

Potential Positive Impacts
- **An easier time keeping up with payments, leading to a positive payment history.** If a cardholder has multiple credit card balances to transfer, they will only have one credit card bill to pay rather than several once the balance transfer is complete. This, plus low or no interest, can help keep the cardholder on track. On-time payments are critical to good credit. At 35%, payment history is the most significant FICO Score factor.
- **An increased credit score because of a lower credit utilization ratio.** Credit utilization is represented by a percentage and measures how much revolving credit a borrower is using compared to how much they have available to them. Imagine you have two maxed out cards, each with a $5,000 limit. Then, you transfer these balances to a balance transfer card that has a

$15,000 limit. You keep your older cards open. Here's how that would affect your credit utilization ratio.

Before the transfer:
- Total balance: $5,000 (card one) + $5,000 (card two) = $10,000
- Total credit limit: $5,000 (card one) + $5,000 (card two) = $10,000
- Credit utilization ratio: $10,000 balance ÷ $10,000 limit = 100%

After the transfer:
- Total balance: $10,000 moved to balance transfer card (card three)
- Total credit limit: $5,000 (card one) + $5,000 (card two) + $15,000 (card three)
- Credit utilization ratio: $10,000 ÷ $25,000 = 40%

A credit utilization score between 1% and 7% is ideal, but most lenders consider 30% acceptable. Although 40% is higher than these figures, it's still a lot better than the 100% credit utilization you had prior to the balance transfer. Credit utilization plays a major part in the amounts-owed FICO Score factor, which makes up 30% of a score.

COMMON BALANCE TRANSFER PITFALLS

Balance transfers can be a savvy way to consolidate debt and pay less total interest. But once the transfer is complete, the process can't be undone. If not handled correctly, the cardholder could end up in a worse financial position. We'll cover some common mistakes consumers make before, during, or after a balance transfer. Knowing these can help you avoid a costly headache later.

Acquiring Debt on Other Cards after the Transfer

Balance transfer cards are a tool that can help borrowers get out of credit card debt faster and with less interest. But borrowers are not required to close their old cards once balances have been transferred. In the best case scenario, these cards should be left open to avoid shortening the borrower's credit history. If borrowers do keep these cards open, however, they should limit their use to very occasional charges (just enough to keep the issuer from deactivating the card) until their balance transfer card is paid down. Transferring a balance without slowing down spending is a common way to perpetuate the cycle of debt.

Failing to Pay the Full Balance Before the Intro Period Ends

If a borrower doesn't pay off their balance by the end of their intro period, whatever they have left over is subject to interest from the time the intro period ends onward. This isn't as financially harmful as what can happen with deferred interest cards. With those, interest is backdated from the date of the original purchase if there's a leftover balance when the intro period ends. Still, balance transfer cards tend to have high rates once the balance transfer period is over. Depending on how much the borrower has left to pay—and how long it takes them to pay it—there's potential for a significant amount of additional interest.

Using a Balance Transfer Card to Pay

Borrowers can still make regular purchases on balance transfer cards, even if that's not the card's true intended use. However, purchases made on a balance transfer card don't usually get a grace period on interest like on a traditional card. Instead, interest will start accruing from the date of purchase at the card's regular purchase rate (not the balance transfer rate). With a traditional card, interest doesn't apply unless the borrower fails to pay off their full balance by the end of their billing cycle. **It's best to keep balance transfer cards separate from cards you use for purchases.**

Making a Late Payment

Paying late on a balance transfer card could cause the issuer to eliminate the card's low- or no-interest introductory period. When this happens, not only might the cardholder lose their intro period, but the issuer might apply a higher-than-normal penalty APR. At best, paying late and losing the intro period defeats the purpose of a balance transfer card. At worst, the borrower could be left in a worse position due to high interest charges and late fees.

Chapter 8

How Credit Impacts
Major Life Purchases

If you've read much of the book up until this point, you now understand how credit scores work and how they're calculated. Now, it's time to learn how credit can impact your day-to-day. Your score can affect your life in ways you might not realize: It can dictate how much you pay for car insurance, whether you need to put down a deposit when turning on utilities, and, in some cases, whether you get a job.

Good credit opens doors, and bad or no credit slams them shut. In this chapter, you'll go behind the scenes to see exactly what happens after you submit that loan or credit card application. You'll also learn how lenders use your score to price out different types of loans and how you can leverage good credit to get a better rate.

LOAN UNDERWRITING

A Peek Behind the Curtain

When you apply for a loan or credit card, your application goes through a process called underwriting. This can be conducted by a loan underwriter (a person who manually reviews your financial and credit history) or through an automated underwriting system, which uses software and algorithms to assess risk and make fast decisions. Either way, underwriting is a critical step that helps lenders decide whether to approve your application, how much credit to extend, and what interest rate to offer you.

THE FIVE CS OF UNDERWRITING

From lender to lender and product to product, underwriting isn't uniform across the board. Different financial institutions have different risk appetites, internal policies, and proprietary models. Some banks might be more conservative, focusing heavily on income and debt-to-income ratios. Online lenders might be more lenient and willing to approve borrowers with less-than-perfect credit.

Still, the principles behind underwriting are generally the same. Lenders are essentially asking: Is this person likely to repay the money we lend them, in full and on time? An easy way to understand the basic principles of underwriting is through the five Cs:

- **Conditions:** Lenders use market conditions to decide how tight their overall guidelines are. For instance, when the job market is soft, lenders may tighten up their eligibility requirements because of a higher risk of the borrower being laid off.

- **Credit history:** Lenders evaluate applications using the borrower's credit score, payment history, bankruptcy history, and more, including how long the borrower has had credit (and which kinds they have held).
- **Capacity:** Capacity measures the applicant's ability to pay back what they borrowed, based on how much they earn and how much debt they currently owe. Lenders look for borrowers with stable sources of income, so job tenure may also play a role.
- **Capital:** Lenders favor applicants with capital—cash, investments, savings, physical assets—as these can indicate financial responsibility. Plus, capital provides a safety net for the lender, which knows that even if the applicant loses their job, they should have the means to pay because they have a nest egg.
- **Collateral:** Collateral helps boost loan approval since the lender can make back some of its losses through repossession. Collateral only makes a difference on secured loans, like mortgages, auto loans, and home equity lines of credit (HELOCs).

If the person is on the favorable end of these five Cs, they're more likely to get the loans they're after.

WHAT HAPPENS AFTER YOU APPLY?

The loan process varies greatly depending on the type of loan or credit you're applying for. Some loans are straightforward, like credit cards and personal loans. For these, you usually only need to fill out an online application and upload basic documents like a government-issued ID. Mortgages, on the other hand, are much more involved and typically require years of W-2s and months of bank statements. That's not to mention an appraisal, which is a way for the lender to underwrite the property instead of the borrower. Here's what happens after a borrower applies for a loan or a card, generally speaking.

The Application Is Screened by a Computer System

Most applications go through an automated underwriting system (AUS) before a human gets involved. An AUS is a software program or AI algorithm that can give an instant or near-instant credit decision based on the lender's underwriting factors. An AUS for a credit card issuer that only accepts good credit will automatically reject applicants with sub-670 FICO Scores, for instance.

Different Lenders, Different Rates

How is it possible to get varying rate offers from multiple lenders, using the same information? Overlays (on mortgages) or internal guidelines (on other loans and cards). Think of these as scoring metrics. As long as they don't break the law, lenders are free to choose their own metrics and how they are weighted.

The AUS often works in tandem with other information gathering programs to confirm factors like the applicant's employment status and credit history. Based on what it finds, the AUS may approve the applicant and move them to the next stage of the underwriting process, or it could conditionally approve the application but flag information that needs additional scrutiny from an actual underwriter, reject the application, or refer the application to an underwriter because it was unable to make a decision based on the information available.

The Application Is Reviewed by a Person

If the AUS approves or conditionally approves the application, the application may be moved on to a human loan processor or underwriter for further review. At this point, the applicant may need to provide supporting documents, like a government-issued ID to prove their identity, a home appraisal in the case of a mortgage, or proof of insurance for auto loans. Assuming the underwriter issues approval, they will send the application through the lender's pricing engine. This software uses the applicant's information as well as the lender's overlays or internal guidelines to determine what rate to offer.

The Applicant Signs Paperwork

If the applicant accepts the offer, they will sign paperwork (a promissory note for a loan or a contract for a card). This paperwork outlines annual percentage rates (APRs), interest rates, fees, terms, and other rules and definitions. This paperwork is legally binding, so it's essential that the applicant read and understand what they are signing. The applicant will also make their down payment when signing, if one is required (like in the case of an auto loan or mortgage).

USING A LOAN TO BUY A CAR

Get Behind the Wheel by Borrowing Smart

Unless you have enough cash to pay in full, you're going to need a loan if you want to buy a car. Many car buyers let the dealer handle their financing. After all, the dealer is the expert, so you might as well sit back and let them do all the legwork, right? Wrong. The dealer may be able to find you the best deal on a car loan. However, you can't know for sure until you explore your options—and how your credit dictates what options may be available to you.

FACTORS OTHER THAN CREDIT THAT IMPACT CAR LOAN RATES

Credit scores play a significant role when it comes to car loan rates, but they aren't the only factor. Auto loan rates also depend on:

- **Whether you're buying used, new, or are refinancing:** In general, new car loans have the lowest rates, followed by used cars and auto loan refinancing.
- **The length of your loan term:** The longer it takes to pay off a loan, the more opportunity the borrower has to fall behind. Lenders charge higher interest on longer terms to make up for this extra risk.
- **Loan-to-value ratio:** Loan-to-value ratio (LTV) measures how much of the car you are financing compared to its worth. An LTV over 100% is a red flag for lenders. If the lender has to repossess

the car, it knows that whatever the car gets at auction won't be enough to cover the loan. High LTVs can happen if the car buyer doesn't make a down payment, rolls warranties and other extras into their loan, or finances an older, cheaper car. Higher LTVs lead to higher rates, if the borrower is approved at all.

- **Down payment amounts:** The more a borrower puts down, the less they must borrow. This demonstrates financial responsibility.

TYPES OF CAR LOANS

As with other types of loans, car loans come in different types. The following outlines some of the most popular.

Manufacturer Financing

Manufacturer financing (or captive financing) is when the carmaker provides an auto loan; an example is Toyota Motor Credit. Captive car loans can come with perks like low- or no-interest financing, rebates, and cashback incentives. These deals are most commonly found during major holidays and at the end of the year. These help dealers sell older inventory to make room for next year's models.

Manufacturers rarely disclose their credit score requirements. Instead, these loans are only available to "well-qualified buyers." This typically means at least good credit (670+ for FICO Scores), an acceptable debt-to-income ratio, and more. As long as you're shopping at an authorized dealer, you can apply for manufacturer financing on the lot. Otherwise, apply online.

Indirect Financing

Most car dealers work within a third-party lender network in order to set people up with auto loans. This is called indirect financing. With this, the car buyer will fill out a loan application at the dealership. Then, the dealer will use the application to shop for a loan on the car buyer's behalf. To serve the largest number of customers, dealers usually have a wide range of lenders within their network—including those that specialize in bad credit, good credit, and everything in between.

Indirect financing can be convenient since the dealer does the loan shopping. However, there's no guarantee that the dealer will show you the loan with the lowest rate. Of course they want to make a sale, so they aren't going to price you out. But they could pick a loan with a slightly higher rate if it means an extra kickback for them. If you're considering indirect financing, do some loan shopping first to make sure that what the dealer offers you is better than a loan that you can get on your own.

Beware of Dealer Reserve

As an incentive, lenders typically allow dealerships to mark up interest rates by 1–3% through something called dealer reserve. The dealership pockets this difference as profit. Dealer reserve isn't shown on your paperwork. You'll have to ask about it directly or avoid it by securing your own financing.

Bank, Credit Union, and Online Lender Financing

Banks, credit unions, and online lenders can also be great places to get an auto loan—banks and credit unions especially, as they carry lower rates. However, banks and credit union auto loans can be hard to qualify for unless you have strong credit. Online loans can come with higher rates or more fees.

Buy Here, Pay Here Financing

A buy here, pay here car loan is funded by the dealership itself. These car loans often take advantage of borrowers with lower scores by charging astronomical rates and fees. Find out more in the "Predatory Lending" entry in Chapter 4.

THE PERKS OF PREAPPROVAL

Getting preapproved car loans can help you find the best rate and can be a powerful negotiating tool. Once you know what car you want, follow this simple list:

1. Go online and get preapproved for about five car loans. Shop with a few different types of lenders, including manufacturers, banks, credit unions, and online lenders.
2. When you're at the dealership, find out what kind of loan the dealer can offer you.
3. Toward the end of the process, show the dealer your lowest preapproved car loan and ask them to beat it (assuming the dealer's loan isn't best). Dealers make money on financing, so they may go the extra mile to find a lower rate.

For more information on preapprovals, please see the entry "Hard and Soft Credit Inquiries" in Chapter 2.

UNDERSTANDING PERSONAL LOANS

A Loan You Can Use for Almost Anything

U.S. residents owe more than $250 billion in personal loan debt, and that number is steadily increasing. Even so, personal loans typically make up the smallest amount of consumer debt overall when compared to mortgages, car loans, and credit cards—less than 2%, according to Federal Reserve Bank of New York data from the third quarter of 2025.

Good credit or bad, most borrowers qualify for a personal loan. Payday loans and tribal loans are a type of personal loan, and these loans don't require a hard credit check. In exchange for an easy loan, these lenders charge exorbitant rates and fees. However, not all personal loans are made alike. For people with strong credit, a personal loan can be one of the cheaper ways to borrow money. At least compared to credit cards.

WHAT IS A PERSONAL LOAN?

A personal loan is a type of installment loan, like mortgages and auto loans. But instead of the money going directly to the entity or person selling property, the lender sends the money to the borrower (in most cases), usually by direct deposit. Personal loans have fixed interest rates and as long as the borrower pays according to their payment schedule, the amount of interest they owe will not grow over time like it would with a credit card. Monthly payments also remain the same over the life of the loan.

Personal Loan Uses

Lenders place very few restrictions on how their personal loans can be used. Borrowers usually can't use a personal loan for post-secondary education (due to heightened regulations around student loans), investing, gambling, or illegal activities. Other than that, personal loans are typically fair game. One of the most popular reasons people get a personal loan is to consolidate credit card debt. Borrowers also commonly use personal loans for high-dollar projects like home renovations or for emergency expenses.

When Can a Personal Loan Make Sense?

A 0% APR credit card is perhaps the best way to borrow money, but only if the borrower qualifies and can pay off their balance during the introductory period (usually six to twenty-one months). This strategy means free credit, unless the card has some other fee. If the borrower needs years to pay off their debt, then a personal loan will likely make more sense. Credit card interest compounds and personal loan interest doesn't.

Personal Loan Rates versus Credit Card Rates

If you have excellent credit, personal loan APRs are about 5–7% cheaper than a credit card. But bad credit can mean triple-digit interest rates. By most standards, loans with rates higher than 36% are predatory.

Further, a personal loan may be a better fit for someone who has a large, up-front purchase with an end price tag. Personal loans come as a lump sum, and once the money is gone, the only way to get more is to take another loan. If the borrower doesn't know exactly how much they'll need (or if they'll need to borrow over time), they'll likely find more benefit with revolving credit like a credit card, HELOC, or personal line of credit.

Common Personal Loan Features

- **Unsecured:** Most personal loans don't require collateral, but some lenders offer it as an option for lower rates or easier approval. Online lenders typically use the borrower's car as collateral, and banks/credit unions may use a savings or investment account.
- **More expensive than secured loans:** Personal loan APRs are higher than home equity loans and HELOCs. The latter use your home as collateral. This reduces the risk for the lender and, in turn, the borrower's interest rate.
- **No down payment:** Unlike auto loans and mortgages, personal loans never require a down payment. A lender may charge an up-front fee, but it will usually take it out of the loan itself rather than ask for it out of pocket. Lenders that charge out-of-pocket fees for a personal loan (like an application fee) should be scrutinized—this is a sign of predatory lending.
- **Wide range of loan amounts and repayment terms:** Personal loans can be big or small, from a few hundred dollars to a few hundred thousand dollars. Borrowers typically get 12–60+ months to pay the loan back.
- **Can have an origination fee:** Some personal loans can come with an origination fee, especially those obtained online. An origination fee is usually a percentage of the requested loan amount, and the borrower typically deducts it from the loan before sending the borrower their money.

CREDIT REQUIREMENTS
FOR A PERSONAL LOAN

There's a personal loan lender for practically every credit type. That said, personal loan rates usually don't start getting competitive until the borrower has a good FICO Score (670+), and borrowers need very good credit (740+) to get a lender's best rates, sometimes higher. Getting a personal loan with bad credit is possible, but these loans are very expensive. Non-predatory bad-credit lenders cap their rates at 35.99%. This is still quite high, especially on longer loan terms. Borrowers pay more overall interest the longer their loan is active. It's always a good idea to use an online personal loan calculator before signing on the dotted line to truly understand how much the loan will cost you over time.

Just like any other loan, though, personal loan lenders look at more than a borrower's credit score when reviewing their loan application. You could have top-notch credit and still be denied for a personal loan if you earn a lower income or have a short payment history. How much debt the borrower already has is also important. Personal loan lenders want to see a debt-to-income ratio below 30%, although those that specialize in bad-credit loans can accept higher.

MORTGAGE CREDIT REQUIREMENTS

How to Call a House a Home

Buying a home is the biggest purchase most will ever make, and big purchases require big loans. Specifically, mortgages. Mortgages are one of the most complicated loans to get approved for. Truthfully, learning everything you need to know about mortgages could take its own book. But in this entry, you'll learn how mortgage lenders evaluate creditworthiness.

MORTGAGE CREDIT SCORES

There are dozens of different scoring models, but which one do mortgage lenders use? They calculate their own mortgage-specific score, typically using a combination of Fair Isaac Corporation (FICO) models from each of the three credit bureaus. To get these scores, mortgage lenders pull something called a tri-merge credit report. A tri-merge report combines information from all three major credit bureaus:

- Equifax's mortgage-specific score is called Beacon 5.0, which is based on FICO Score 5.
- Experian's mortgage-specific score is called Experian/FICO Risk Model v2, which is based on FICO Score 2.
- TransUnion's mortgage-specific score is called TransUnion FICO Risk Score 4, which is based on FICO Score 4.

If the homebuyer is applying by themselves, then the mortgage lender will usually take a median of these three scores and use that to determine the homebuyer's mortgage credit score. When the homebuyer has a co-borrower, the lender pulls all three scores for both applicants and uses an average of each borrower's median score.

Shifting Regulations Make Homebuying More Accessible

In 2025, the Federal Housing Finance Agency announced that mortgage lenders can use VantageScore 4.0, a more lenient scoring model. Whether lenders choose VantageScore over FICO Score is up to them. If they do, they would get VantageScores instead of FICO Scores from the three bureaus.

OTHER WAYS MORTGAGE LENDERS DETERMINE CREDITWORTHINESS

Just as with other loans, mortgage lenders evaluate much more than just the applicant's credit score. Lenders want to make sure that, holistically, the potential homebuyer is financially responsible and capable of making their mortgage payments. Along with credit scores, mortgage lenders also review:

Debt-to-Income Ratio (DTI)

DTI measures how much the applicant earns compared to how much debt they already have. DTI is an important underwriting factor for just about any loan, but it's especially important in mortgage lending. In fact, some types of loans (usually personal loans) only consider one type of DTI (back-end), while mortgage lenders look at two.

The first type is front-end ratio, sometimes called mortgage-to-income ratio; this considers how much of an applicant's income would go toward the home expenses—not only the mortgage but also property taxes, homeowner's insurance, and homeowners' association fees—if the lender were to approve them. Front-end ratios help make sure that the homebuyer won't become "house poor" after buying their home. Front-end ratios should be 28% or lower.

When lenders disclose their DTI requirements, they're usually referring to the second type: back-end ratio. Back-end ratio compares an applicant's income with their current debt. Debt here includes housing expenses (current rent or mortgage), auto loan debt, personal loan debt, credit card debt, student loans, child support, and alimony. DTI (front- or back-end) does not include non-debt payments like groceries and utilities. Back-end ratios should be 35% or lower, although lenders do generally accept higher.

Mortgage Reserves

Mortgage reserves are cash and/or assets that the applicant can fall back on in case they lose their income stream. Basically, it's a sort of "insurance" for the lender that the applicant will be able to pay their mortgage for some time in the event of job loss. Mortgage reserves can be cash in a bank account, retirement accounts, life insurance policies, and other assets. How much the applicant must have depends on factors like the type of mortgage they're applying for, the applicant's credit score, their DTI, and the lender. Importantly, the applicant doesn't have to give mortgage reserves to the lender. They only must prove that the reserves exist.

Job Stability

Typically, applicants need to prove two or more years of current work history. Lenders do give some wiggle room here to accommodate for unique situations. For instance, if the applicant took time off to care for a sick family member or due to an illness of their own, the lender may make an exception. However, to make up for a lack of work history, the applicant may need to make a larger down payment, have stellar credit, or have a cosigner.

Down Payment Amount

A larger down payment reduces the risk for the lender. The more the applicant puts down, the less they have to borrow and the more they will lose if they default. Making a larger-than-required down payment can help an applicant get approved if they fall short in other areas. Bigger down payments also typically mean lower interest rates.

Loan Repayment Term

With car loans, it can be harder to be approved for a longer repayment term because it gives the borrower more time to fall behind. Mortgages can work backward. Mortgages typically run from fifteen to thirty years. Fifteen-year mortgages can be harder to qualify for because payments are much higher than they are on thirty-year mortgages, simply because there's less time to spread the balance across. These higher monthly payments could push the applicant's front-end DTI in the wrong direction.

CREDIT REQUIREMENTS FOR SPECIFIC MORTGAGE LOANS

Which One Is Right for You?

Now that we've gone over what a potential homebuyer needs to qualify for a mortgage in general, it's time for a quick overview of the types of mortgage loans available—and what it takes to qualify for them. Mortgages are a long-term financing product that typically last for fifteen to thirty years. Unless you refinance later, you'll keep the same mortgage loan you initially chose when you first bought your house. Knowing your options is key to picking the financing that's right for you.

CONVENTIONAL LOANS

Conventional mortgage loans are issued by private mortgage lenders and are the most common type of mortgage. But within conventional mortgages sit two subcategories: conforming and nonconforming.

Conforming Conventional Loans

A conforming conventional mortgage is one that meets, or conforms to, Freddie Mac and Fannie Mae requirements. Freddie Mac (technically the Federal Home Loan Mortgage Corporation) and Fannie Mae (the Federal National Mortgage Association) are government-sponsored enterprises (GSEs). They don't issue mortgage loans themselves. Remember, conventional loans are always issued by private mortgage lenders. Instead, Freddie and Fannie back certain mortgages with the help of the U.S. government.

GSEs are a bit confusing. Freddie and Fannie are not technically arms of the federal government (they are private companies owned by shareholders), but they operate under government control and oversight. This is because the government has deemed them too big to fail. The Great Recession showed the world what could happen if such a large sector of the U.S. mortgage banking system was not backed by the government: a national housing market crash.

Conforming conventional loans generally have lower interest rates, lower down payment options, and first-time homebuyer and special loan programs, as well as transparent eligibility requirements. This makes these mortgage loans appealing to those that can get them. To qualify for a conforming conventional loan, both the homebuyer and the property must meet certain requirements.

Property Requirements

- **Home value:** Varies from year to year and is based on the average home values in the area.
- **Appraised value:** The home appraisal must meet or exceed the sale price.
- **Home condition:** Must be livable, safe, and structurally sound.
- **Property type:** Can be a single-family home, two-to-four-unit multifamily dwelling, townhouse, or condo.
- **Use:** Must be for residential purposes only; no agricultural or business use.

Private Mortgage Insurance (PMI)

PMI is required on conventional loans when the homebuyer puts less than 20% down. PMI protects the lender, and it is an extra expense tacked on to the mortgage. Homebuyers can ask their lender to remove PMI once their principal balance hits 80% of what they paid for the home.

Borrower Requirements

Homebuyers themselves also need to meet certain eligibility criteria to qualify for a Freddie or Fannie loan. Each entity also offers their own homebuyer programs, with their own separate requirements. For instance, Fannie Mae's HomeReady® program allows for a lower down payment and cheaper PMI premiums, but only for low-income homebuyers. Freddie Mac's Home Possible® program typically requires a higher credit score than HomeReady®. Until recently, Fannie Mae required a 620 credit score for HomeReady® (it has since removed its credit score requirements). Freddie Mac's Home Possible®, however, requires 660. Also note that while Freddie and Fannie have their own underwriting criteria, so do the lenders that these government programs work with. These lender-specific requirements are called lender overlay. That means homebuyers must not only meet Freddie's and Fannie's requirements, but also those of the lender that is writing the Freddie or Fannie loan. In general, though, homebuyers must meet the following guidelines to qualify for Freddie or Fannie:

- **Minimum credit score:** Varies by program for Freddie Mac; no minimum for Fannie Mae (historically, it was 620 but this minimum was eliminated in late 2025)
- **Maximum debt-to-income ratio:** 36–45%
- **Bankruptcy:** At least four years since a Chapter 7 discharge; at least two years since a Chapter 13 discharge

If these guidelines are met, you're more likely to be approved.

Nonconforming Conventional Loans

Nonconforming loans are ones that do not meet Freddie or Fannie requirements, and eligibility guidelines vary from lender to lender. For example, mortgage lenders that specialize in jumbo loans (or extra-large mortgages) will only accept the most qualified borrowers. Other lenders that primarily work in the subprime market might accept borrowers with credit scores that are too low for Freddie or Fannie.

NONCONVENTIONAL GOVERNMENT-BACKED LOANS

A nonconventional government-backed loan is a mortgage that is insured by the Government National Mortgage Association, otherwise known as Ginnie Mae. Unlike GSEs Freddie and Fannie, Ginnie is a government agency, not a private company. These types of mortgages aim to help those who can't qualify for a conventional mortgage to buy a home, or they give special benefits to people who belong to a certain group or are buying in a specific area.

Federal Housing Administration (FHA) Loans

Rates for FHA loans are typically lower than conventional mortgages, but they come with their own specific expenses, including an up-front mortgage insurance premium (UFMIP) and an annual mortgage insurance premium (MIP). The former is a percentage of the loan amount that is rolled into the mortgage balance. The latter is a percentage of the loan amount tacked on to the homebuyer's monthly mortgage payment. These take the place of PMI. Some of the eligibility requirements for an FHA mortgage include:

- **Minimum credit score:** 500
- **Minimum down payment:** 3.5% (for credit scores 580+); 10% (for credit scores 500–579)
- **Maximum debt-to-income ratio:** 43%
- **Loan limits:** FHA loans are capped to a certain amount, and this amount changes each year

Assuming all of these are met, you may qualify for this loan type.

U.S. Department of Veterans Affairs (VA) Loans

Only certain military members, veterans, and surviving spouses can get a VA home loan. Military members also need to be enlisted for a specific period to qualify. VA loans tend to carry low rates, and PMI isn't required. However, they do have a VA funding fee, which can equal 0.5–3.3% of the total loan amount. Here are some of the requirements for VA loans:

- **Minimum credit score:** No set minimum, but many lenders require a score of at least 620
- **Minimum down payment:** 0%
- **Maximum debt-to-income ratio:** 41%
- **Loan limits:** If the borrower has a full entitlement from the VA, no limit applies (for more information, please contact the VA or a Veterans Service Officer)

Assuming all of these are met, you may qualify for this loan type.

U.S. Department of Agriculture (USDA) Loans

USDA loans are for lower-income borrowers that are buying a home in a rural area and can't qualify for a conventional loan. There are three different types of USDA loans. The following information pertains to USDA direct loans:

- **Minimum credit score:** Typically 640, but can be lower depending on other factors
- **Minimum down payment:** 0%
- **Maximum debt-to-income ratio:** 41%
- **Loan limits:** Varies by county

Assuming all of these are met, you may qualify for this loan type.

Native American Direct Loans (NADLs)

NADLs are for eligible Native American veterans enrolled in a federally recognized tribe. Non–Native American veterans married to a Native American can also qualify. The home must be located on federal trust land. NADLs do not require PMI, but there is a similar funding fee of 1.25%, though this can be waived under certain circumstances. Here are some requirements for NADLs:

- **Minimum credit score:** None, but still must prove to be an acceptable risk
- **Minimum down payment:** None
- **Maximum debt-to-income ratio:** 41%
- **Loan limits:** No set limit

Assuming all of these are met, you may qualify for this loan type.

CREDIT SCORES AND INSURANCE RATES

The Link Between Credit Score and Claims

Your credit score can have a huge impact on how much you pay for auto and homeowner's insurance. According to FICO, about 95% of auto insurers and 85% of home insurers use credit as a factor when determining premiums in states where credit-based insurance scoring is allowed. On the surface, it might not seem fair. Just because someone has a lower score doesn't automatically make them a bad driver. But insurance is all about risk, and actuarial data shows that drivers with lower scores are more likely to file a claim.

HOW CAR INSURANCE COMPANIES CALCULATE RATES

If you've had car insurance for any length of time, then you probably have experienced premium fluctuations through no fault of your own. This is due to how insurance generally works. Insurance companies take policyholders who share certain rating factors, group them together, and analyze their claim frequency. A rating factor is some aspect about a driver or their car that has a hand in how an insurance company calculates a rate. Driving history, the type of car someone drives, and where they live are all examples of rating factors. If a group of policyholders has a higher likelihood of filing a claim, then all drivers in that group will have higher premiums. For instance, let's say that accident frequency went up in your zip code. In that case, your car insurance premium could increase even if you didn't have any accidents or tickets, just because the area you live in is now a higher risk.

CREDIT-BASED INSURANCE SCORES

In most states, insurance companies use credit-based insurance scores as a factor when determining premiums. A credit-based insurance score isn't the same thing as a standard credit score. For one, reviewing an insurance-based credit score only results in a soft credit pull on a credit report, so shopping around for insurance won't impact your credit score. Also, the factors that FICO uses to calculate a credit-based insurance score aren't exactly the same as what it uses for a traditional FICO Score. Credit-based insurance scoring factors are as follows:

- Payment history (40%)
- Outstanding debt (30%)
- Length of credit history (15%)
- Pursuit of new credit (10%)
- Credit mix (5%)

At 40%, payment history is slightly more important on a credit-based insurance score than it is on a standard FICO Score (where payment history accounts for 35%). Credit mix also varies a little, as this factor makes up 10% of a FICO Score and only 5% for a credit-based insurance score.

As long as the factor isn't considered unfair discrimination, it's largely up to the state insurance department (not the federal government) to regulate insurance scoring factors. A handful of states have either banned credit-based insurance scoring or have set restrictions on its use. These states include California, Hawaii, Maryland, Massachusetts, Michigan, Oregon, and Utah.

Isn't Age a Protected Class?

Younger drivers typically pay higher rates because statistics show that younger drivers are more likely to get into an accident, even though age is a protected class. For this reason, insurance carriers are allowed to use age as a rating factor. Other protected classes, like race, color, national origin, and religion, have no statistical correlation to accident risk.

THE DATA BEHIND CREDIT-BASED INSURANCE SCORES

Car and home insurance carriers began to use credit-based insurance scoring in the early 1990s, but how much weight a credit-based insurance score carries in a particular company's underwriting model is considered a trade secret. As a result, there isn't much publicly available data that shows the correlation between credit-based insurance scoring and accident frequency and severity. However, studies done over the past few decades have shown that drivers with lower credit-based insurance scores typically file more auto and homeowner's insurance claims, and that those claims are generally more expensive than those filed by policyholders with higher scores.

CREDIT-BASED INSURANCE SCORING CONTROVERSY

Car and homeowner's insurance companies charge higher rates for lower scores because there is a statistical link between lower scores and claim frequency/severity. Even though the numbers correlate, is using someone's credit score to determine their car or home insurance premium fair? Some consumer advocacy groups say no. They argue that:

- **Someone can have bad credit because of an unavoidable life event.** Perhaps the policyholder got sick or was laid off, leading to financial difficulties. Is it right to penalize a policyholder for something outside of their control?
- **Credit-based insurance scores could unfairly target minority groups.** Using race as a rating factor is illegal. But could credit-based insurance scoring indirectly lead to higher premiums for minority groups due to income disparity?
- **Using credit as a rating factor punishes people with little or no credit.** Some people willingly choose to avoid debt and credit. Others are just starting their credit journey. Does that necessarily mean that they are a less responsible driver or homeowner?

With these factors in mind, it may be more difficult to argue in favor of using a person's credit score to determine rates. But if we don't use this metric, what should be used instead?

KNOWING WHEN TO REFINANCE A LOAN

Swap That Old Loan for a New One

When a borrower signs a loan agreement, they're locked in until that loan is paid off—unless they refinance. Refinancing is the act of swapping an old loan for a new one, hopefully with better rates and terms. This entry examines what refinancing is, why someone would consider doing it, and the potential risks refinancing can carry.

WHAT DOES IT MEAN TO REFINANCE A LOAN?

Refinancing a loan is the act of taking out one new loan and using it to pay off one older loan. Once the refinancing is complete, you'll begin to pay the new loan rather than the old loan—the old loan no longer exists, as it was paid off with the refinance loan. People refinance for a few reasons. Refinancing allows you to remove a co-borrower, lengthen or shorten your loan terms, and/or save money on interest through a lower rate.

Imagine this: You bought your car two and a half years ago. At that time, your credit score was 680. Good, but not great (at least in the eyes of FICO). You have an APR of 8% on your auto loan. One of your goals since you've purchased your car has been to improve your credit score, and you did! You got a higher-paying job that allowed you to pay down some of your current debt, and some old late payments fell off your credit report.

Today, you're boasting a solid 780 score. You think that you might qualify for a better rate on your car loan. You shop around for auto loan refinancing and are approved for a new loan at 5.20% APR. You agree to the loan, your refinance lender pays off your old loan for you with your new refinance loan, and you start making payments on your new refinance loan moving forward.

Don't Let a Payment Slip Through

Refinancing takes a lot of moving parts, and it usually doesn't happen over-night. Car loans, for instance, usually take around forty-five days from start to finish. It's essential that you continue making your current loan payments until you're certain that the old loan is closed.

WHAT'S THE POINT OF REFINANCING?

Although the specific previous example paints a picture of auto loan refinancing, the general idea is the same for most installment loans (such as mortgages and personal loans). Why do people refinance loans? For some, it can help reduce interest rates (like in the car loan example). It can also:

- **Lower the borrower's monthly payments:** The borrower can either get a lower interest rate, if they qualify for one, or choose a longer loan term. A longer loan term allows the borrower to stretch their balance over more time (so, lower monthly payments, but higher overall interest).

- **Help the borrower pay the loan off faster:** Refinancing to a loan with a shorter term will squeeze the borrower's balance into a smaller window of time. This will help them pay off the loan faster and save interest, but it means their monthly payments will be higher.

- **Remove a co-borrower from the loan:** Unless the current loan has a cosigner or co-borrower release, the only way to remove a second person from a loan is to refinance it with a new one in only the borrower's name.

- **Help the borrower access cash:** A cash-out refinance (a type of refinance loan) allows the borrower to replace their loan but also take out some of their equity (how much something is worth minus how much they owe) as cash. So, the borrower will take out a refinance loan that's bigger than the loan that they are refinancing. Cash-out refinancing mostly applies to mortgages, but it is also possible on auto loans.

Is It Worth Trying to Time the Market to Refinance?

The economy is volatile, so don't try to time the market. Concentrate on what you can control—your credit score. Make payments on time and pay down debt. With dedication, your credit score should go up and the refinance rates you qualify for should go down.

WHAT TO CONSIDER BEFORE REFINANCING

Refinancing can be a great way to save money and find a loan that better fits your needs, but it isn't magic. Refinancing does have some downsides to consider.

Fees

Loans come with fees, refinance loans included. Refinancing a mortgage typically requires closing costs of 2–6% of the amount being refinanced. The borrower's current loan may also have a prepayment penalty. These aren't too common, but some lenders charge a fee for paying off a loan early. When a borrower pays off a loan faster than their payment schedule dictates, the lender will make less in interest.

Loss of Equity If Cashing Out

Although you can use the cash from a cash-out mortgage refinance for just about anything, this strategy can be a great way to fund home renovations, which in turn should increase the value of the home. However, borrowing against equity also means you own less of the home and owe more to the bank.

Restarting the "Clock"

Unless the borrower chooses a loan term that exactly matches how much time they have left on their current loan, refinancing essentially undoes the progress the borrower made on their current loan. More time in debt means more total interest.

Chapter 9

Protecting Your Credit and Identity

When you get a data breach notification in the mail, do you shrug your shoulders, say "oh well," and get on with your day? If so, you wouldn't be alone. Data breaches are so common that it's sometimes hard to take them seriously. There's even a term for this phenomenon: data breach fatigue. But it's so important to fight that fatigue. Identity theft can be devastating, emotionally and financially. With just one slipup, criminals could gain access to your most personal financial information, ruin your credit, and leave you to pick up the pieces. It takes a lot of work and time to build and maintain good credit—protecting it is essential.

The best way to solve a problem is to prevent it in the first place. That's what this chapter is about. You'll learn how to lock down your credit, the different types of identity theft, and common scams to look out for. With this information, you might even feel comfortable enough to skip that pricey credit monitoring service which, in all honesty, probably isn't worth it anyway.

IDENTITY THEFT

Protecting Yourself Means Knowing the Signs

Many people's first foray into identity theft is getting their debit or credit card stolen when shopping online. Unfortunately, that's not the only kind of identity theft there is. There are dozens of different types of identity theft, but they all have the same purpose: to use someone's good name to obtain credit, a job, or government benefits, or for some other personal or financial gain.

Identity Theft Costs Us Billions

Year over year, the Federal Trade Commission logs millions of identity theft and fraud complaints. In 2024 alone, Americans reported losing $12.7 billion because of these two issues combined.

CLUES THAT POINT TO A STOLEN IDENTITY

It can take years to recognize that your identity has been stolen. This is especially true in the case of child identity theft. With these, the victim doesn't typically realize that their identity has been stolen until they apply for their first loan or card, after they come of age. But most often, there are immediate signs that something is amiss. You might be a victim of identity theft if you have:

Unexplained Bank and Credit Card Activity

For many, a call or text from their bank or credit card's fraud department is the first sign that their identity has been compromised. Financial institutions use algorithms and software to track account holder spending habits. If the fraud department detects activity that doesn't match the account holder's usual patterns, it will flag the transaction and block it until it has been confirmed that it is the account holder making the purchase. Ask your bank or card about its fraud prevention policies and check your statements on a regular basis to look for suspicious activity.

Data Breach Notifications

Having your information leaked in a data breach doesn't guarantee that your identity has or will be stolen. It does put you at higher risk, however. Most companies that experience a data breach offer free credit monitoring services to those affected. Consider taking advantage of it for extra peace of mind.

Unexpected Debt Collection Calls

Identity thieves can rack up a ton of debt if you don't catch the problem quickly enough. In this case, you might get calls from creditors attempting to collect debt that's in your name but that you didn't actually approve.

Rejected Tax Returns or Unexplained Tax Documents

Some identity thieves fraudulently file other people's taxes in order to steal the returns. When this happens, the Internal Revenue Service (IRS) will reject the victim's tax return because, in its eyes, it's a duplicate request. Receiving unexplained tax documents can be another tip-off that your identity has been stolen. For instance, if you're a salaried employee but you receive a 1099 (a form reserved for independent contractors), you should double check your credit report.

Correspondence about Unexpected Unemployment Benefits

It's not uncommon for identity thieves to steal information so they can apply for unemployment benefits under a different name.

Explanation of Benefits for Unreceived Medical Treatments

Legally, health insurance companies must send an explanation of benefits (EOB) after each claim they handle. Getting unexplained EOBs might mean that your identity was stolen so someone could receive medical treatment or prescription drugs.

Change of Address Notice

Getting a change of address notice from the post office or other entities could potentially mean that a criminal is trying to reroute your mail to steal bank statements or other sensitive information.

Password Reset Emails for Online Accounts

A flurry of password reset emails is an indication that someone may be trying to hack their way into your online accounts. When you can, always set up two-factor authentication as an extra layer of protection.

TYPES OF IDENTITY THEFT

There are many different types of identity theft that may occur, including:

- **Financial:** Financial identity theft occurs when the thief steals the victim's information in order to get a loan or credit card or to sign up for services.
- **Tax:** Some thieves steal Social Security or employment identification numbers so they can steal other people's tax refunds.
- **Medical:** This type of identity theft allows the thief to steal prescription drugs or obtain medical treatment using the victim's information.
- **Child:** When it comes to credit, minors have a blank slate. This makes them a prime target for identity thieves. In these instances, the thief uses the child's information to get a loan or card, ruining the child's credit before they've had the chance to build it.
- **Senior:** On the opposite end of the spectrum, some criminals specifically target senior citizens so they can steal their Social Security check and/or other benefits.
- **Estate:** If a thief steals a deceased person's information to open accounts, that's estate identity theft.
- **Social Security:** Some criminals steal Social Security numbers in order to get a job using someone else's identity.
- **Friendly or familial:** Since they have easier access to your information, it's possible that a friend or family member could steal your information to apply for a loan or credit card. This is especially common between parents and children.
- **Synthetic:** Synthetic identity theft happens when a thief uses a combination of real and fake information, or more than one person's real information, to create a new identity.

- **Biometric:** Some criminals steal people's fingerprints to unlock devices and gain access to sensitive information.
- **Property:** Also known as title fraud, property identity theft happens when a criminal steals your personal information and transfers the deed to your house to someone else, likely themselves or an accomplice.

Be vigilant, as you never know what kinds of people are out there potentially affecting you or your loved ones.

WHAT TO DO IF SOMEONE STEALS YOUR IDENTITY

Act Fast to Minimize Damage

You just received a notification that someone changed the password to your online banking account. But there's a big problem: You didn't request it. Now is time for action and damage mitigation. Following the steps throughout this entry—swiftly and thoroughly—can help you recover from identity theft faster and, hopefully, for good.

HANDLING A STOLEN IDENTITY

The following are steps you should take in order if you've received some level of credit theft:

1. **Contact a credit bureau and place a fraud alert.** A fraud alert tells lenders and credit card companies that you may be a victim of identity theft. As a result, they must take extra steps to verify your identity, making it harder for the criminal to borrow using your name. Because you only need to contact one bureau versus all three, alerts are faster than freezes. The fraudster could be applying for multiple lines of credit immediately, and a fraud alert can quickly cut them off at the pass. We'll discuss the difference between fraud alerts and freezes in the entry "Credit Freezes and Fraud Alerts" later in this chapter.

2. **Call your bank.** Ask your bank to deactivate your debit card, credit card, and/or checking account numbers so that the criminal can't syphon funds from your account.

3. **Report the identity theft to the FTC.** This step establishes a paper trail, and after providing details about the incident, the Federal Trade Commission will create a personalized recovery plan for you to follow. Report your case to www.identitytheft.gov.

4. **Freeze your credit.** Contact all three credit bureaus to freeze all of your credit reports. Legally, the bureaus must complete the freeze within one business day of your request if the request was done online, or three days for mailed requests.

5. **Change all passwords.** Next, change the passwords to your online banking, social media and any other accounts that contain sensitive information or can help the fraudster more easily impersonate you. Consider signing up for multi-factor authentication while you're at it.

6. **File a police report.** Contacting the police after your identity has been stolen is optional but recommended. The report you filed with the FTC serves as legal proof that your identity has been stolen, but a police report can help strengthen your case when contacting lenders. It's unlikely that a police report will lead to an arrest (unless you know the thief), but a police report allows you to place an extended (seven-year) fraud alert on your credit reports. A standard fraud alert remains in place for one year, with the option of renewing.

7. **Call companies and service providers.** If you found out about your identity theft through a new, unexplained line of credit or loan, call the lender immediately. Explain that your identity

has been stolen and that you did not request the loan or card. They will guide you through next steps.

8. **Review your credit reports and dispute fraud.** What you've done so far should stop your current identity theft case from escalating and prevent future incidents. Now it's time to assess and mitigate the damage. Order reports from all three bureaus and carefully examine them line by line. Pay particular attention to new tradelines. If you find any that you did not request, call the lender or card issuer immediately and file a dispute with the bureaus. See the entry "Disputing Errors on Your Credit Report" in Chapter 5 to learn more.

Create a Personal Fraud File

Having your identity stolen is emotionally violating. After all, a stranger has gained access to your most personal information. Keeping a detailed fraud file might help you feel more in control. Send disputes by certified mail and record important details of every related conversation you have with lenders.

After you wrap up these steps, continue to watch your accounts. Freezing your credit should stop anyone from opening new accounts in your name, but only if the loan or card they apply for runs a traditional credit check. Payday loans, for example, don't require a credit check. They won't appear on your credit report unless you default. Then, the lender sells your debt to a collection agency, at which point the loan will be added to your credit report.

PROTECTING YOUR INFORMATION IN A DIGITAL WORLD

Keeping It Clean with Internet Hygiene

Nearly three-quarters of adults in the United States have been a victim of an online scam or cyberattack, according to the Pew Research Center. The most common crime? Debit and credit card number theft—almost half of those surveyed reported fraudulent charges.

The victims here aren't to blame. Criminals these days have highly sophisticated methods of gaining access to your most sensitive information. Still, there are steps you can take to put a proverbial padlock on your financials.

MANAGING PASSWORDS AND LOG-INS

Passwords are the keys to your kingdom, and boy, do we have a lot of keys. Americans juggle an average of 168 passwords per NordPass, a password management software company. Knowing this, you must take steps to protect your log-in info. Weak passwords and sloppy password management can make you an easy target for fraudsters and thieves.

Password Best Practices

Have you ever reused log-ins and passwords across multiple platforms? You wouldn't be the only one—but that doesn't mean that it's a good idea. By doing so, you run the risk of losing access to multiple accounts due to a single data breach. When creating a password, you should:

- **Make them complicated.** Even if they are harder to remember, your password should not be a complete phrase, name, date of birth, or anything else "sensical." Instead, create complex passwords that have a mix of numbers, letters, and symbols. Passwords should be at least fourteen to sixteen characters long.
- **Make them unique.** As mentioned, do not recycle passwords for different accounts.
- **Consider a password manager.** A password manager is essentially an encrypted password vault. When you save a password to your password manager, the password gets encrypted (or scrambled into code). Then, those encrypted passwords are sent to the password manager's servers for safekeeping. Instead of keying in passwords for each individual account, you will use one master password (the one to your password manager) to log in. Password managers can also auto-create complex passwords when you sign up for a new online account.

Following this advice will keep your information safer.

Enable Two-Factor Authentication (2FA)

Two-factor authentication forces you to provide two pieces of identifying information (such as a personal identification number or your thumbprint) before you can log in to certain accounts. You can find 2FA software programs and apps online, just be sure to use ones offered by reputable companies, such as Microsoft. You may also have the option of turning on 2FA if it's built into your cell phone or email hosting site.

HOW TO SPOT PHISHING

Phishing is an attempt to steal passwords, account information, and identities through fake emails and other communications. These communications often contain links to ransomware, which hackers use to lock up your computer. Then, the hacker will demand payment to unlock your computer or to stop them from leaking your sensitive info. Phishers typically pose as someone the victim knows, like a loved one or a boss. To avoid getting hooked in a phishing attack, you should:

- **Check the sender's email address.** If the email domain is spelled wrong (such as gmaile.com instead of gmail.com), it's likely a phishing attempt. Also, make sure that business emails you receive were sent through a corporate email address and not a public one, like Gmail or Outlook.
- **Look for suspicious language.** Bad grammar and spelling can be a phishing sign, especially if the email is supposedly coming from a professional organization. Also see if the language pattern makes sense if the sender claims to be someone you know.
- **Be unflustered by "urgent" requests.** Phishers often pose as authority figures and give arbitrary timeframes and outsized consequences to get you to comply.
- **Be skeptical of requests.** Don't blindly follow orders if you get a strange request. For instance, if someone claiming to work in your company's human resources department asks you to send or verify sensitive information, refuse and speak to HR directly.

Phishing is more and more common every day in both personal and professional settings, so make sure you keep an eye out.

Types of Phishing

Phishing has been around for almost as long as household internet itself. The first known phishing attack occurred in the 1990s, when hackers impersonated AOL employees and breached users' instant messages and emails to steal passwords. But as the internet evolved, so did tactics. Today, phishing can be split up into several categories:

- **Smishing** uses text messages instead of emails.
- **Quishing**, or QR phishing, helps hackers steal information through fake QR codes.
- **Vishing** is phishing through scam phone calls—the v stands for "voice."

Have You Ever Received an Unexplained Package?

If you've received something you didn't order, you may have been a victim of brushing. Brushing is when online retailers send unsolicited packages of cheap products to unsuspecting recipients. Then, the seller writes a fake review under the recipient's name. Free stuff might seem cool, but it also means that your sensitive information may be compromised.

AVOIDING COMMON SCAMS

The Best Defense Is a Good Offense

Americans lose billions of dollars annually due to fraud and scams. The FTC reported that consumers lost over $12.5 billion to fraud in 2024 alone. This is a 25% increase, compared to 2023. In this digital age, you must stay skeptical and learn how to spot common scams to protect your credit score and your wallet. This entry helps arm you with the information needed to do just that.

GOVERNMENT IMPERSONATION SCAMS

Government impersonation scams take advantage of people's fear of authority, or trust of authority, depending on the context. These fraudsters claim to represent a government agency to separate consumers from their money. Some government impersonation scams to watch out for include:

- **Jury duty:** Hang up immediately if you get a call from someone claiming to be law enforcement or threatening legal action or fines for failing to report to jury duty. After, contact your county courthouse to see if you missed a jury duty letter.
- **Social Security:** The Social Security Administration will call consumers if there's a business reason to do so. However, it will

never ask for your Social Security number or personal details, threaten you, or demand payment.

- **Medicare:** Medicare will never contact you to pressure you to change plans, cancel your coverage, or to let you know that you are entitled to free equipment or refunds.

Any of these should cause your internal scam sensors to go off.

ONLINE AND TECH SCAMS

Online and tech scams capitalize on a lack of computer knowledge. Some of these scams are easier to spot than others, but no matter your comfort level with the online world, never put your guard down. Tech scams to watch out for include:

- **Tech support:** With a tech support scam, a criminal claims to be from Microsoft, Geek Squad, or another software or tech support system. They attempt to convince the victim to buy their services when, in reality, they are collecting bank account information.
- **Fake website:** Some websites look real but are designed to trick consumers into keying in their account information. Look for the padlock icon and "https://" next to the website's URL. This doesn't guarantee the site is real, but it can help. Real websites should look professional and be free of most, if not all, grammatical errors.
- **Online rental ad:** With these, scammers will place a fake ad for a rental home or apartment, usually at a very low price. Addresses and photos are often real, but the property is not owned by the scammer posing as the landlord. When the prospective tenant

shows interest, the scammer explains that they are out of town but will hold the place with a security deposit. Once the victim sends the deposit, the landlord and listing will disappear.

These scams are prevalent throughout online channels, so keep your mind clear, and if something looks too good to be true, it probably is.

FINANCIAL, INVESTMENT, AND EMPLOYMENT SCAMS

Financial, investment, and employment scams appeal to people's natural urge to make money. According to the FTC, investment scams cause consumers the most monetary damage compared to any other category.

Crypto and Stock Scams

If someone you don't know offers to show you how to make money with crypto or stocks, do not engage. The same is true if you're offered some sort of rebate or perk for downloading a stock or crypto app. It's perfectly fine to take investment advice from trusted parties (as long as you do your research), but not from online strangers.

Multi-level Marketing

While not technically illegal, multi-level marketing (MLM) is the contemporary version of a pyramid scheme. If you're considering a job that hinges on you signing up recruits (or downlines) to sell with you rather than selling actual product, you're likely looking at an MLM.

How Many People Actually Make Money Through MLMs?

The FTC estimates that 99.6% of people who sign up for an MLM lose money, as most programs require up-front product purchases. Skin care, essential oils, athleisure wear, and makeup are popular MLM products.

Job Offer Scams

Job offer scams often take advantage of those desperate for work. If you get a cold call or email from a recruiter and something doesn't seem right, end the conversation and contact the company directly. Look for bad grammar, odd email addresses, and virtual interviews conducted by chat versus video call. You should also never have to pay up front to apply.

Check Cashing Scams

Check cashing scams go hand in hand with employment scams. Here's a common scenario: Your new "employer" sends you a check to reimburse expenses. However, the check is for more than the agreed-upon amount. The employer instructs you to cash the check and wire them the difference to make things right. What you don't realize is that the check is going to bounce in a few days after the wire has gone through.

EMOTIONAL SCAMS

Emotional scams prey on people's loneliness, empathy, or the love they hold for family and friends. Seniors are especially vulnerable, but emotional scams can happen to anyone.

Pig Butchering

This scam is as ugly as it sounds. Pig butchering often starts with a text that seems like it was intended for someone else. Then, the messenger will slowly strike up a friendship with the victim. Once trust has been gained, the scammer will rope the victim into sham investments or otherwise convince them to send money.

Online Romance Scams

Most people have heard of the Nigerian prince scam, but online romance scams are often more nuanced. The scammer may send pictures and video to prove their identity, but there's no guarantee that the person is romantically interested in the victim or that they are who they say they are. Never send money or gift cards to someone you haven't met in person.

Kidnapping and Arrest Scams

These scary scams often target older parents and relatives. A criminal contacts the victim pretending to be the person's child, grandchild, or another loved one. The caller says that they're in some sort of trouble, usually kidnapped or arrested. Then, the criminal asks for bail money or ransom.

CREDIT FREEZES AND FRAUD ALERTS

Putting Your Credit on Ice

According to a 2022 study from the Consumer Financial Protection Bureau, 86% of credit card applications are completed online or via mobile app. Borrowing money at home on your own time is no doubt convenient, but it does make it easier for people to impersonate you and get a loan. Freezing your credit is a quick, free way to stop thieves from using your good name to apply for loans and credit cards.

WHAT IS A CREDIT FREEZE?

A credit freeze prevents lenders and card issuers from pulling your credit report when they receive a loan or card application. When your credit is frozen, no one—not even you—can apply for a new loan or card. Freezing your credit is free and a legal right granted under the Fair Credit Reporting Act.

If someone applies for a loan or card while your credit is frozen, the lender will stop the process by declining the application or by putting it on hold until your credit is unfrozen. Credit freezes aren't infallible, though. Debt collectors have access to frozen credit reports, as do current creditors. It also only protects you from possible future incidents. Even so, it's best practice to keep your credit frozen unless you're shopping for a loan. Credit card and loan fraud can be financially devastating.

FREEZE/UNFREEZE YOUR CREDIT

You must contact the bureaus individually to freeze and unfreeze all three of your credit reports. Though annoying because you must manage log-in info, you can always get a password manager to help with this (see the entry "Protecting Your Information in a Digital World" in this chapter), but generally, freezing and unfreezing a credit report takes a few minutes by phone or online or a few days if through paper mail.

Equifax
- Visit www.equifax.com/personal/credit-report-services/credit-freeze
- Call (888) 298-0045
- Download a security freeze request form from Equifax's website (https://assets.equifax.com/assets/personal/Security_Freeze_Request_Form.pdf) and mail it to: Equifax Information Services LLC, P.O. Box 105788, Atlanta, GA 30348-5788

Experian
- Visit www.experian.com/help/credit-freeze
- Call (888) 397-3742
- Send a written request along with your name, Social Security number, date of birth, addresses for the last two years, and copies of your ID and a utility bill or bank statement to: Experian Security Freeze, P.O. Box 9554, Allen, TX 75013

TransUnion
- Visit www.transunion.com/credit-freeze
- Call (800) 916-8800
- Send a written request, along with your name, address, and Social Security number to: TransUnion, P.O. Box 160, Woodlyn, PA 19094

Locking Your Social Security Number

Consider locking your Social Security number with the Social Security Administration by visiting www.e-verify.gov/employees/mye-verify. This won't stop someone from using your Social to get a loan or card, but it can prevent your name from being used to fraudulently obtain employment.

WHAT IS A FRAUD ALERT?

Along with credit freezes, the Fair Credit Reporting Act also grants consumers the right to place a fraud alert on their credit reports. A fraud alert indicates to lenders that the applicant may be a victim of identity theft. This red flag legally requires the lender to take extra steps to confirm the applicant's identity, usually by phone, before moving forward. The same is true when a lender receives a credit limit increase from an existing cardholder with a fraud alert.

There are three types of fraud alerts, and all of them are free. Consumers only need to inform one bureau, and that bureau will inform the other two (unlike a credit freeze, which requires contacting all three). The first fraud alert is an initial fraud alert; this lasts a year, but you can choose to renew it. The second type is reserved for victims of identity theft; these last for seven years and require an identity theft report with the FTC or a police report. They're renewable if the consumer resubmits the report. The last type is an active duty alert, which last for one year, and they can be renewed throughout a service member's deployment. All types can be helpful in their own ways.

BENEFITS OF CREDIT FREEZES

Compared to fraud alerts, credit freezes are a more reliable way of keeping fraudsters from racking up new debt in your name. Credit freezes essentially lock down your credit, while a fraud alert flags it, advising lenders that the application requires closer scrutiny. But what happens if the criminal has enough information to impersonate you over the phone? Or what if the lender misses the fraud alert? A credit freeze would put a stop to these scenarios.

Still, the safest thing would be to place both a credit freeze and a fraud alert on your credit file. Two layers of defense are better than one, and both options are free.

CREDIT FREEZES VS. FRAUD ALERTS		
	CREDIT FREEZE	**FRAUD ALERT**
What It Does	Blocks access to a credit report	Requires lenders to take extra steps to verify an applicant's identity
Effectiveness	Very effective, as it places a hard stop on your credit file	Less effective, as a criminal may impersonate the applicant during verification
Actions Needed When Applying for Credit	Must manually unlock with each bureau	Must provide extra identity verification to lender
Who to Contact	All three credit bureaus	Just one credit bureau

CREDIT MONITORING

Is It Worth Paying For?

There are dozens of credit monitoring services out there. Some are free, but most require a subscription, which can cost hundreds of dollars a year in monthly fees. This entry aims to help you figure out if these paid services are worth it based on your unique needs.

CREDIT MONITORING SERVICES

A credit monitoring service is a company that monitors credit reports for changes, like new hard credit inquiries. If it detects a change, it will notify its client. By doing so, the client can take quick action if they weren't the one to trigger the change.

Free credit monitoring is bare bones. The company may only monitor one bureau instead of all three (Equifax, Experian, and TransUnion). The service will also likely come with ads along with loan and credit card offers. Ads are what make the service free. The paid version comes with more benefits and other identity-theft-related services. Naturally, the more features a service has, the more expensive it is. When comparing services, look at:

Monitoring Cadence

Some services monitor a client's credit report continuously. With any change, the credit bureau notifies the monitoring service, and the monitoring service notifies the client quickly. Other companies may go weeks or months between checks.

Types of Credit Scores Provided

Credit monitoring services usually provide credit scores. Free services often just provide VantageScores, while paid also provide FICO Scores. Some may even give specific FICO Scores, like for auto or mortgages.

Cybersecurity Tools and Dark Web Monitoring

Some elaborate services offer online identity protection with VPNs or password managers; some even scan the dark web for personally identifiable information (PII) like your Social Security number. Though potentially expensive if you're already paying for identity protection elsewhere, it could be cheaper to roll them all under a credit monitoring service.

Fraud Restoration

If a client's identity is stolen and they carry fraud restoration, the credit monitoring service will help recover the client's information and restore their identity by calling creditors or contacting credit bureaus. Some monitoring services even keep licensed private investigators on staff for this reason. In these cases, the client may give the investigator power of attorney to take some of the pressure off of the client.

Recovering from Tax Identity Theft

Identity restoration can take a long time, but it depends on what kind of damage the thief did. The IRS reports that it can take more than a year and a half to resolve tax identity theft, although its goal is four months.

Online Reputation Management

A few companies count online reputation management among their services. Here, the credit monitoring company will review their clients' social media accounts and digital footprints to make suggestions on how their clients can clean up their online personas.

Identity Theft Insurance

Identity theft insurance can be bought as a stand-alone product from many insurance companies, but some credit monitoring services provide it too. This coverage may also pay out if the client suffers a financial loss related to data breaches, fraud, and more.

IS CREDIT MONITORING WORTH IT?

Credit monitoring can certainly be a helpful tool, but keep in mind that it won't stop a thief from stealing your identity—it only alerts you if it happens. Then, you're left to deal with the aftermath, sometimes with the credit monitoring service's help.

For most people, paid credit monitoring isn't necessary. You have the power to stop criminals in their tracks for free. Remember the following steps and be careful out there.

1. **Freeze your credit reports.** When a credit report is frozen, all hard credit inquiries attempted on that report will be blocked. Although you'll have to unfreeze your credit if you apply for a loan, line of credit, or credit card, the process typically takes just a few minutes and may protect against loan and card fraud.
2. **Place a fraud alert with the bureaus.** A fraud alert is a flag to lenders that you may be a victim of identity theft. So, they

are legally obligated to take reasonable steps to verify your identity before issuing credit. This usually entails a phone call from the lender's fraud or underwriting department.

3. **Safeguard your Social Security number.** You can lock your Social Security number with the Social Security Administration. This can prevent fraudsters from using your Social to get a job and/or commit tax fraud under your name.

4. **Check your credit score and reports regularly.** Everyone is entitled to a weekly free credit report from each of the three credit bureaus. Check them often so you can spot suspicious activity quickly if needed. And while most free credit scores are VantageScores (although lenders typically use FICO Scores during underwriting), they're still a good way to keep an eye on your overall financial health.

In the end, there's no universal right answer when it comes to free or paid credit monitoring. Some are at higher risk of identity theft, like those who've already had their data stolen and sold on the dark web. These people may find the paid services worth it, while others might not be able to avoid the price tag. Examine any personal risks to make the choice right for you.

INDEX